Women on the line

Ruth Cavendish

Women on the line

Routledge & Kegan Paul
London, Boston and Henley

First published in 1982
by Routledge & Kegan Paul Ltd
39 Store Street,
London WC1E 7DD,
9 Park Street,
Boston, Mass. 02108, USA and
Broadway House,
Newtown Road,
Henley-on-Thames,
Oxon RG9 1EN

Set in Journal Roman by
Academic Typing Service, Gerrards Cross, Bucks
and printed in Great Britain by
St Edmundsbury Press, Bury St Edmunds, Suffolk

Library of Congress Cataloging in Publication Data

Cavendish, Ruth, 1946-
Women on the line.
1. Women automobile industry workers –
England – Case studies.   2. Assembly-line
methods – Case studies.   I. Title.
HD6073.A82G73   305.4'3   81-13907

ISBN 0-7100-0987-9   AACR2

Contents

Freedom of speech

This book is based on my personal experience of working on the assembly line in a factory in a major English town sometime during the period 1977–8. The factory is a real one and the product is an essential component of every single vehicle on the road. When I first wrote up my account, I took care to invent names for all the women I had worked with, so as to protect them against possible victimisation by the company. I also changed the names of all the other people mentioned so that they would not be personally identified. However, I deliberately left in the name of the firm; there is very little direct information available about working conditions and production processes in particular industries and companies in Britain, and next to nothing about how these affect women workers. My aim was to give concrete facts about the factory, placing it in the local employment structure and in the motor and motor components industries, and to write about a specific group of workers and the struggles they are faced with. I wasn't attempting an exposé of the factory – there must be countless others with equally bad pay and conditions; nor was my aim to point a finger at any particular company.

This was very naïve, as it turned out. If the firm was named, there was a risk both to me and to the publisher that the firm might bring a libel action against us. British libel laws place the burden of proof on the author. I would have to be able to prove legally that everything I said about the factory was true. On the other hand, to win the action and prevent distribution of the book, the firm need only deny my statements; they would not need to disprove them.

Lawyers outlined the two possible ways open to me of proving that what I said was true. One would be to substantiate my facts by referring to already published material – for obvious reasons there is none. The other way would be to call on witnesses to back me up. But it would be quite wrong to put the women I worked with in such a position, and would doubtless guarantee them the sack in any case.

Several lawyers were consulted and all agreed that I must rewrite the account so as to make the firm unidentifiable. Some interpreted the law more restrictively than others, and some publishers were less willing than others to take even the slightest risk. The upshot of all this is that I have been obliged to disguise the firm, its location, and product. The delay between 1978 and publication is due to sorting out the libel issue.

I decided to call the company Universal Mechanical and Electrical Components Limited (UMEC) and have checked that no such company is in fact registered at Companies House. What I say in chapter 2 about the company and its place in the motor industry is based on its actual company accounts and on published reports, but I have altered them sufficiently to make the company unidentifiable. I cannot quote my references because that would give the game away.

The factory is now located in West London, which is not true, and I have invented a name for the near-by trading estate, now known as the Victoria Trading Estate. I had to omit the names of all the companies with factories operating on this trading estate, which has affected chapter 9 and chapters 1 and 7 to a lesser extent. They are all well-known companies, producing goods with brand names familiar to everyone.

To name the particular motor component we manufactured would be tantamount to naming the firm so I have taken rather extreme steps to disguise that too. While some people are concerned to identify flying objects, I've been legally constrained to make unidentifiable an everyday and well-known object – hence 'unidentifiable mechanical objects' or UMOs for short. I have retained the names of commonplace components (covers, cases) and common operations (electrical checking, packing) which you would find in the production of many goods other than UMOs. However, I've invented names for any subcomponent that could possibly identify a UMO. This has affected chapter 3 considerably, where a nonsense product is described as being assembled from nonsense parts. As far as I know, there is no such thing as a diactor, module or silicone. Operations like calibrating torque and screwing down transistors are intentionally gobbledegook. Giving the components fictitious names enabled me to preserve my detailed account of the work process. I hope that this is still of interest despite the loss of work content.

Finally, the trade union representing the women workers: its name also had to be invented, because of the risk of possible libel action from a right-wing union and/or its local branch officials or regional officers. It is now called the Industrial Workers and Technicians Union (IWTU). I've also omitted the names of all the other unions on the site which represented different groups of workers. The account of the dispute in chapter 8 is true except for the names of the parties involved.

When I first wrote up my diary, I had no idea how restrictive the libel laws are, and learnt the hard way. I would much rather have kept in all the names and all the concrete detail. As it is, I have preserved as much as I could and hope that what has been lost in detail is compensated for in a small way by making clear the extent of the legal constraints on freedom of speech. As an individual, one is helpless to challenge the libel laws. It would take collective organisation – in this case, it would mean having decided together with all the women on the shopfloor that we wanted to take on the company in this way. But this is totally unrealistic: it's not the way the women would go about things, and they have far more important matters to sort out.

British libel laws protect especially those institutions and people in established positions of power. I have been forced to go to great lengths to protect the name of the company and to make it unidentifiable. The book itself now stands as evidence of the limitations on freedom of speech and who benefits from those limitations.

Ruth Cavendish

Chapter One
A factory job

I had been thinking of taking a working-class job for years before I actually went to work in the factory. I had a host of reasons for doing so, both personal and political. Basically they represented a wish to put my feet on more solid ground. I was a product of the 1960s student movement, formed politically and intellectually by involvement in struggles over education, the Vietnam and other anti-imperialist movements, and by the Women's Liberation Movement. I'd been active in many groups but never joined any of the left-wing groups or parties.

By the mid-1970s I felt that the sort of politics I'd been involved in was approaching an impasse. I'd stayed on in higher education, taken a higher degree and had been teaching sociology at university and polytechnics for eight years. But conditions had changed drastically since the early days. Student struggles now centred on the grants issue. There was little criticism of course content or questioning of how education perpetuates class divisions. My possible political activity was increasingly restricted to union politics over teachers' conditions and the education cuts. Even teaching Marxism and courses on racism and women's oppression seemed like a contradiction: students could just regurgitate radical lectures in their exam papers without any change of political outlook. As academic sociology became more parasitic on Marxist and feminist theory, books and topics which had been taboo in 1970 now became required reading, and in the process lost much of their critical impact.

At the same time many intellectuals in Britain had retreated from active political involvement into academic

Marxism. They seemed to be delving further and further back into the 'theory of theory', worrying about how to construct concepts, and criticising one analytical framework in terms of another. This retreat into theoreticism seemed arid and abstract to me. Keeping a distance from ongoing struggles might further the philosophy of science, but it didn't contribute much to our understanding of the decline of capitalism on a world scale, or of economic and political forces in Britain today.

Many left-wing intellectuals come from a middle-class background and hold professional jobs – they enjoy sufficient income and spare time to cushion them from the harsh realities of life experienced by the majority of workers. Trying to keep one's feet on the ground and have a concrete grasp of ongoing working-class struggles had always seemed to me an antidote to a middle-class lifestyle, essential if we were to understand the people on whose behalf we were supposedly theorising. Yet recent theories had revelled in the longest of words, and the most abstract of analyses, with a disregard and even arrogance for working-class people and their everyday problems.

The socialist 'wing' of the women's movement was losing some of its earlier dynamism. We'd never properly succeeded in one of our main aims – to contact and involve working-class women. Was it the demands we made or the way we organised that failed to attract them? Individual feminists had contact with working-class women over housing, childcare and health issues, and many feminists in their capacity as social workers had working-class clients. But there was little opportunity to meet working-class women on an equal footing; as many of us were young, professional and single, our experience of life was quite different from that of our working-class sisters.

My job and politics were limited and frustrating. In some ways, 'movement' politics seemed to be a leftover from the late 1960s and early 1970s when we could choose to organise around education, sexuality and other issues not 'at the point of production'. Since then economic crisis has brought us sharply face to face with the nitty-gritty of economic issues, and working-class struggles at the point of production have returned to the forefront of the political arena. The other issues are not peripheral in the least but we need to find ways to link them with the concrete realities of class in Britain today.

So I was looking for a new way of being involved politically, where I might have daily contact with working-class women over the long term. Learning from them would help me appreciate their experience and understanding of life from the inside for a change. Friends of mine had taken routine office jobs or hospital work, but I decided to look for factory work. I had no experience so it would have to be unskilled or semi-skilled, like the work done by the vast majority of women manual workers; and I was expecting the very low pay – 'married women's wages' – characteristic of such work.

I didn't know much about the employment structure in West London where I lived, and walked round the local trading estates to look for a job. I was surprised to see that most of the women workers in the largest trading estate, which I shall call Victoria Trading Estate, were of Caribbean or Asian origin – few factories had even a small proportion of white women. It would be difficult enough for me to be accepted by working-class women, but I was worried that the barriers would be that much greater if I was one of the few whites. Black and Asian women would have more reasons to be suspicious of me, on account of my colour as well as my background, education and speech. It would be easier to fit in where there were some other white women.

I decided on Universal Mechanical and Electrical Components Limited (UMEC), a large factory some distance from Victoria Trading Estate, which employed mainly women, black, white and Asian. The factory manufactured a component for the motor industry – the 'unidentifiable mechanical object' or UMO.*

Getting the job itself was straightforward; I was interviewed in the personnel office and offered clerical work.

---

* In 'Freedom of Speech' I've explained why I have had to give the factory a fictitious name and location, and also disguise the nature of the product.

I said I'd prefer manual work, and they gave me the choice of operating one machine or working on the assembly line. The line would give closer contact with other women so I chose that. The supervisor took me round the workshop and told me about pay and conditions. My being an ex-teacher didn't seem to worry them, but they were surprised that I turned down the cleaner, better-paid clerical job. After I'd had a medical and provided a reference, they told me to report for work the following Monday. I could see from the brief guided tour that all the assemblers were women, and that the work was very fiddly and fast.

I worked at UMEC for seven months in 1977–8. At the beginning, my intentions were open-ended; if I fitted in and thought I could become involved with the women in the factory and in the community, I was prepared to make it a long-term commitment. But there was no telling in advance how I'd stand up to the hard physical work and long hours, and I was worried that the women wouldn't accept me. I'd also have to manage on the low wages. Although I'd been an active socialist feminist for a long time, my outlook must have been influenced by my own experience – of a relatively well-paid job with short hours and long holidays, and by being single and childless. I wondered whether the very different experience meant that the central issues in the women's movement were not so relevant to working-class women, and if others were more important.

In addition to trying to answer these broad questions and the attempt to be politically involved in a different way, I hoped that working in a large factory would help me think about particular questions of class analysis. Nowadays the working class is much more differentiated than it was a century ago; the vast majority of workers are wage labourers who sell their labour to an employer in exchange for a wage; there are far fewer self-employed, domestic servants and rentiers than in the past. Developments in technology and more mechanised methods of production require workers with different degrees of skill and education, and a whole array of white-collar administrative, scientific and clerical personnel. The state itself has become a major employer over the last few decades. Laundering, food preparation and other work which used to be done in the home is now carried out on a capitalist basis outside the home, and accounts for the vast expansion of the female service sector. These changes have resulted in a labour force, differentiated into many types and levels by different degrees of skill and education, who enjoy widely varying work conditions and wage levels. What are the similarities and differences between the different groups? What forces divide them and what would encourage them to ally?

Some recent Marxist analyses take the fact that both top scientists, say, and night cleaners are wage labourers to be the common denominator, outweighing the differences between them. Others distinguish between sections of the working class on the basis of ideological or political authority given to some groups over others. I thought that much more knowledge and theoretical work were necessary if we were to assess the political implications of this expansion in wage labour. Although all wage labourers fall under the classical definition of the working class, they may have a different relation to production. Is surplus value extracted in a different manner from the different groups? Would this outweigh their common features, and how would it affect their political consciousness? These are not just sociological questions – it is imperative politically to know what specific groupings exist, and what unites and divides them.

My other particular question was about women's work in Britain. How was the expansion of semi-skilled work for women linked historically with the development of more mechanised methods of production? Power-driven machine tools and assembly lines permitted goods to be mass produced by relatively unskilled workers, but our knowledge of how women have been drawn into factories since the 1930s is scanty. Feminists have documented the way women were used to substitute for male engineering workers as a 'reserve army of labour' during the two world wars. We've also analysed domestic labour, women's unpaid work in the home reproducing labour power, and drawn attention to the enormous expansion since 1945 in the employment of married women, part-time women workers and the mushrooming of the service and clerical sectors, the main employers of female labour. However, we know much less about changes in the position of women manual workers – how they have been affected by changes in technology, and deskilling, and what their response has been. We had put forward various reasons for women's pay being so much lower than men's, and drawn attention to their economic dependence. But we hadn't thought much about the links between home and work for low-paid women who work full-time, or how work, home, family and low pay affect each other.

These kinds of questions were at the back of my mind while I worked in the factory and I returned to them after I left. I didn't expect to find the answers there, or expect any thoughts to fall neatly into preconceived categories, but working there gave me some insights and helped me think about such issues. My experience of the work was the same as that of all the other women in the factory and it affected my outside life in much the same way; it was a means of livelihood for me as for them, but I was also observing what went on while they had no pressing need to do so.

My account of the factory and the work is therefore that of an outsider. It is limited because of this, and limited also because I was there for such a short time. It would have taken much longer to come to grips properly with the work process and occupational hierarchy and how these affected the different groups of workers. I tried to find out as much as I could by asking the other women, and by keeping my eyes open but some questions could have been answered only by supervisors or management.

So there may be factual inaccuracies in my descriptions. For example, the women said that the line speed had increased over the years, which may well be true. On the other hand, it may be that the jobs each woman has to do have been enlarged. Similarly, I knew how much we were paid, but only on hearsay how much the autoparts were sold for. We hadn't a clue about the cost of raw materials or components, so I was not in a position to work out the profit margins. I've tried to outline the different grades of men that worked in the factory – engineers, technicians, and so on. Again, this relied on asking people who didn't really care how many different grades of men workers there were; in any case, it took me about six weeks to tell the difference between a progress chaser and a maintenance engineer. After I left, I did some background reading on the motor industry in Britain, and the car components industry, and read up UMEC's company reports.

The idea of writing a book about the factory didn't occur to me while I was working there. To start with, I didn't even keep a diary. After a few weeks I felt as if I'd always worked there, and thought I'd better note things down before I forgot my first impressions entirely. Every week I jotted down what had happened, discussions we had had, stories the women had told, as well as rows with the supervisors. Most of my diary was about how my neck ached and how tired I was. I wrote next to nothing about the actual work or how it was organised. So after I gave up the job I spent a couple of weeks writing in more detail about the work process, how the place was organised and about the relationships between the women. That account forms the basis of this book. Friends read it and encouraged me to write it up more formally – but I was quite reluctant.

Writing a book has the danger of giving more weight than is warranted to one short experience and one particular factory. It would be quite inappropriate to generalise about the lives of working-class women from UMEC. Also I didn't want to betray the friendship and trust of the women by describing them from the outside and risk objectifying them. In the end, I've written it up to show how much I learnt from the women, and how much their friendship meant to me, and hope to make a small contribution to feminist understanding of what life is like for low-paid semi-skilled factory workers.

None of the women ever accused me of dropping in and out of the working class, though I'm aware that this was how it could appear; rather they thought I was 'wasting' my education. But there's no getting away from the fact that someone like me could choose to work in a factory and then choose to give it up – choices not open to other factory workers, and which would always mark off people from an intellectual or middle-class background from those who worked there of necessity.

I was very much in two minds about leaving: I knew how much I would miss the company of the other women, and that in time the work would have become a bit easier for me. The women already wanted me to be shop steward, and if I had stayed it would have been with the intention of working through the union to try and improve conditions. But the union organisation was such that to get anywhere I'd have needed to make it a long-term commitment – five or even ten years. I didn't think I could stand the assembly line that long – repeating the same operations for eight hours day in day out was bad enough after seven months. The job also involved a much greater change in my whole life than I had anticipated. Exhaustion and lack of time made it difficult to come to a major decision like that – there was never a moment to sit back and think it through properly. In the end, I decided to look for another factory where conditions might be a bit better, but, as I explain later on, I couldn't find another job.

For me, working in the factory wasn't dropping in and out – I'd certainly be prepared to do it again and next time I'll know better what to expect. Taking that kind of job must be one of the best ways for feminists to have day-to-day contact with working-class women, and for left-wing intellectuals to establish an active and continuous relationship with working-class people.

Chapter Two

The company

Universal Mechanical and Electrical Components Limited is a large 'multi-business' company with many factories in the UK and employing around 20,000 people. Its turnover exceeded £250m. during the year 1977–8, and £23m. were made in pre-tax profits, an increase of £9m. since 1975. The company holds a major position in the production of UMOs for the UK and is one of the main suppliers to British Leyland and other manufacturers of cars and commercial vehicles. UMEC is one of a small number of companies making auto-parts which hold an effective monopoly in the British motor industry.

According to the company reports, the firms comprising the company manufacture a wide variety of products in addition to components for the motor trade – painting and decorating materials, hydraulic equipment and ventilation systems, and industrial instruments. The firm is in the fore-front of research and development of advanced electronic equipment for the space industry and for medical science, and it has large contracts, both civil and military, for electronic instruments. UMEC manufactures underwater exploration equipment and has pioneered new submarine technology for North Sea oil. Heavy investment in research has paid off in large contracts recently secured with the major companies engaged in these new areas of industry.

The fortunes of the vehicle component side of the company have mirrored fluctuations in the motor industry as a whole. There was a setback between 1974–6 as a result of the three-day week, the energy crisis and rapid inflation but UMEC's profits in vehicle components had recovered from a low of £500,000 in 1975 to over £3m. by 1977.

The general decline of the British motor industry, as well as these ups and downs, has encouraged UMEC to seek larger export markets for their autoparts (particularly in the Common Market), and to diversify production. Manufacture of submarine and electronic equipment uses comparable technology to autoparts, but also suffers from fluctuations in demand. So they have embarked on the manufacture of other products, such as glass and electronic musical instruments, in an effort to secure stable demand independent of fluctuations in the motor and electronics industries, and to even out their profit cycle.

As a major private British company then, UMEC is quite healthy. It owns many factories and manufactures under a large number of trade marks. It has worldwide distribution, and owns subsidiaries in Europe, the USA, Australia, South Africa and elsewhere. Over the last decade, the firm has increased its profitability and succeeded in reducing its workforce, the number of employees falling from 25,100 in 1969 to 19,900 in 1978. The number of individual shareholders fell over the same period: by 1978, 85 per cent of its shares were owned by insurance companies, pension funds, unit trusts and other such bodies.

In the USA and Europe motor manufacturers on the whole produce and assemble their own components, and do not depend on specialist component firms. British motor manufacturers, on the contrary, rely heavily on the independent components firms. The industry has a low level of 'vertical integration': Vauxhall is the most dependent, 'buying-in' 85 per cent of its components, and British Leyland buys-in 65 per cent. This situation gives all the vehicle component firms a central position in the motor industry.

Ford, however, manufactures practically the whole car and then assembles it. Even so, it has turned to 'dual sourcing', attempting to ensure that components are supplied by more than one outlet, so bottlenecks or strikes in one factory won't dry up the source and prevent them assembling vehicles. Other motor manufacturers in Europe are following Ford's example.

In recent years, British components firms have attempted to penetrate the foreign market, and to establish themselves as a dual source for Ford and other companies. This is seen as the only way to offset reduced demand from declining sales of new vehicles in the UK; so exports are a rapidly growing part of the components industry. UMEC has been particularly successful in penetrating the European market – it has contracts with many Continental motor companies and with Ford in Britain. The company has also consolidated its position with British Leyland since the latter was taken into public ownership; Leyland continues to account for a very large, but declining, proportion of UMEC's orders for autoparts.

The site in West London housed UMEC's general headquarters as well as the main factory for the production of UMOs. The place must have been built soon after the turn of the century, and I imagine that UMOs were made there from the early days of the British motor industry. I would guess about 1,800 people were employed in the complex as a whole, about 800 of them on the shopfloor. Apart from the clerical workers, computer staff and the managers, there were engineers, draughtsmen and various grades of craftsmen and technicians, in addition to the manual workers.

As you went through the factory gates, there was a 'road' with buildings flanking either side. On the left, was the large modern office block and computer centre. Then came the factory called 'Assembly 2', where instruments were made for Ford, and the sprocket shop where sprockets for UMOs were assembled. Beyond these was the engineering block which manual workers never entered, and behind it, parallel to a side road, the depot for 'Goods Inwards' where lorries arrived to unload their components for the stores.

On the right-hand side of the 'road', opposite the office block, were the canteens, one for 'staff' and another for manual workers. Then there was a huge block housing the personnel office, first aid, and several of the workshops. The 'machine shop' was in there, and so was the 'spray shop' where metal cases for UMOs were spray painted and the valve shop. The largest shop, the 'main assembly', where I was to work along with all the other women workers, was in there too.

Final assembly of UMOs went on in this main assembly;

the other shops in the factory either made or subassembled components for final assembly. Most of the modules and diactors seemed to be made on the site, as did the basic mechanism for the UMO. Metal cases for lorry UMOs and for the Mini were made in the machine shop, and so were some of the metal clips and lugs. A large number of components came from UMEC's other factories; transistors came from the factory in Scotland, and metal cases for the UMOs for larger cars came from another UMEC factory. Filters for the larger models came by air freight from subsidiaries on the Continent. The remaining components, like screws, nuts and clips, were 'bought-in'.

You could see how all the car firms and their suppliers were dependent on one another. Some of our components came from GEC; we used airguns made by Desoutters, a North London factory that had recently been on strike, and after final assembly our UMOs were whisked off to Coventry or Cowley. Some days we were switched at short notice from one 'set' to another, for instance from Maxi to Marina, because of shortages at Leyland.

UMEC was closely tied in with the fate of the nationalised car industry. The women believed that if they went on strike, British Leyland would come to a halt fairly quickly. Many of them had been laid off in 1977 when the Leyland tool-room men were on strike.

Final assembly was very labour intensive – most of the components were assembled by hand, with the aid of power-driven screwdrivers, and a few simple machines. It was semi-skilled work, done on assembly lines and exclusively by women. At least 200 women worked in the main assembly, on assembly lines running down the length of the shop parallel to each other, each about 30 yards long. There were men too: the chargehands, supervisors, quality controllers and progress chasers but they were standing up or walking around, while all the women sat at benches along the lines. I doubt whether the shop had been renovated in the past twenty years, apart from two new lines for a new Continental UMO built while I was there. In addition to the lines, there was a partitioned-off section on the left of the main assembly where women worked on individual machines, and off on the right there was another small shop where specialist UMOs were individually assembled.

The supervisors sat at the front of the shop in 'boxes', desks which were slightly raised on a platform and fenced off with a wooden partition so the supervisor had a good view over the whole shop. At several points round the side of the shop were the clocking machines and a place for us to hang our coats. There were a couple of Maxpax machines with ready-made tea and coffee. The lavatories were off the shop, right at the back of the lines, and were pretty ancient.

An overhead conveyor system ran right around the shop, transporting what looked like chair lifts. These were for moving out the finished product. The 'seats' dipped down at the end-point of each assembly line, and the last woman on the line lifted up skips containing twelve UMOs onto the 'seat' every few minutes. The skips were carried out from the main assembly through an overhead tunnel and into the 'goods outwards', where they were loaded into lorries and sent on their way to the car factories. Sometimes, if there was a hold-up, the goods outwards men or the lorry drivers would hang around at the back of the lines waiting for their last few skips.

About 70 per cent of the women workers were Irish. Having looked for a factory where there were at least some white workers, I now found I was one of the very few English women there and everyone automatically assumed that I was Irish. About 20 per cent of the women were West Indian, and the remaining 10 per cent were Asian, apparently all from the state of Gujerat in the west of India. Practically all the women had emigrated from their homeland at one time or another and had settled in Britain. A very small number of the young white women were born here of Irish parents or had come with their parents from Ireland as small children and gone to school in West London. But there were no young women of Caribbean or Asian descent born or educated here doing manual work in the factory.

We worked an 8-hour day and 40-hour week, starting at 7.30 a.m. and finishing at 4.15 p.m., with a 45-minute break for lunch at noon. The basic pay was £41 a week, and on top we could earn a maximum bonus of £6. After one year, you were entitled to three weeks' holiday, but you didn't qualify for sick pay for two years. A closed shop operated in the factory, so everyone belonged to a trade union. The Industrial Workers and Technicians Union (IWTU) was the union for the women assemblers. A few weeks after I began work, an industrial dispute started in the main assembly – I'll describe it later.

Chapter Three
Jobs on the line

When I turned up as instructed at the personnel office on the first Monday, the woman in charge gave me a contract as 'assembler', and a clock card number. Then she took me to buy an overall: the firm wasn't responsible for damage caused to our clothes at work, she said. I paid for the overall out of my wages for the next few months at the rate of 20p a week, but never wore it after the first day because the sleeves got in my way. The supervisor collected me and showed me how to clock my card. I must remember to clock three times a day: before we started work at 7.30 a.m., before 12.45 p.m. when we started again after lunch, and at 4.15 p.m. when we went home. Your wages were calculated from the number of hours clocked in, so it's you that suffered if you forgot to clock. Then the supervisor introduced me to Eamonn, the chargehand for the line I was to work on, and they took me to sit with Rosemary, a young Irish woman; I was to sit at her bench and learn the job from her. Rosemary was very friendly – she was pleased to have someone to talk to and share her work, not that I was much help at first. She introduced me to the other women on our line, and to her friends, and showed me where everything was, so I soon felt quite at home, I had no trouble fitting in at all, despite my fears. All the women were friendly and outgoing, which encouraged me to be the same.

From Rosemary's bench you could see everyone in the main assembly, all 200 of them – the women, the charge-hands and supervisors. The shop was light and the women's pink, blue and brown overalls made it quite colourful. You could see which line was stopped, or if there was a breakdown or shortage of components. You could see who the shop steward was talking to. You saw all visitors to the shop, including managers and engineers. You could see who was going to the loo or coffee machine, and how many times a day they went, who was late in the morning, who was clocking out at an unusual time, and who was chatting to whom.

Each line had fifteen 'operators' as we were called, including two 'reject operators' who sat at the end and mended UMOs that were incorrectly assembled or faulty. We sat at benches on each side of the conveyor belt. There was a red light at the head of each assembly line – each time it flashed, every minute-and-a-half or so, the first woman put out a tray containing two UMOs onto the conveyor belt to begin its journey down the line. The conveyor belt itself was only just over a foot wide, and the trays were baskets made of thick dark brown cardboard. A wooden stick was placed across the line at the point where each woman sat, so the tray would come to a halt and she could take out the UMO to do her work. Each time the light flashed, the person in front sent on the tray she had just finished, pushing it over the stick so it would move along the line again, and you sent yours on to the person behind you, so there would be a regular flow of trays.

UMOs were made up from a number of components which we added one by one to the basic mechanism until the UMO was complete. As the trays travelled down the line, each of us added more parts to the UMOs and they became heavier and more cumbersome to handle. By the time the tray reached the end of the line, the UMO was complete: the basic mechanism was covered with modules, sprockets and diactors, and some versions also had three transistors and a filter, each with a cover. Several different versions of UMO were assembled and each version came in a number of models. They were all made from the same basic components but the sprockets, modules and diactors were different for the different 'sets' as we called them. The bulk of the work was for British Leyland and UMOs were assembled for the various Mini, Maxi, Princess, Marina and Allegro models.

My line concentrated on the Maxi and Princess, though

we also assembled UMOs for the Marina and Mini Clubman. We did up to 500 or 1,000 at one go which meant doing the same operations over and over 500 or 1,000 times.

To complete that number took between one and two days. The Princess UMO with its three transistors and filter was much more elaborate than the one for the Maxi. It took longer to assemble so the line went slower, or rather they gave us fewer to do and the light flashed less frequently. Two Maxis travelled down the line in a tray every 100 seconds, so we assembled seventy-two an hour, whereas a tray of Princesses came every two minutes and we did sixty an hour. In fact, though, they both belted down the line so fast that we didn't notice the difference in the light flashing – we'd just be finishing the second UMO when the next lot arrived.

The light was controlled by management who laid down the speed for each set. 'Speeds and feeds' weren't negotiable – we could only query whether the light was flashing more quickly than was laid down, and somebody queried it at least once a day. Each operator had to perform several tasks on the UMO as it made its way down the line. Management was in charge of grouping these jobs, and laid down the number of seconds and split seconds allowed for each. To keep the trays moving at a steady pace, all the jobs ought to have taken the same length of time, but some were harder to complete than others, so there were constant pile-ups. The details of all the jobs were specified on the 'layout', a sheet that Eamonn took out of his desk whenever we switched over to a different set. He walked down the line with it, telling each of us what our jobs were on the next set, and making sure that we were sitting in the right order.

Above the benches hung the airguns, power-driven screwdrivers which we had to pull down to operate. On the bench we had a wooden stand to rest the UMO on, or a mechanical jig to fix it in. There were also plastic cartons of nuts and screws of various sizes, and larger boxes of transistors, modules and so on. The men dragged these along the floor to each bench in large black skips, and sometimes the benches were hidden behind walls of skips and boxes so we could hardly see the women on the neighbouring line.

There was little machinery apart from the airguns and jigs. The calibrating machine for making the sprocket register the correct torque was the most complex. There was a separate machine for checking the calibration, another to check the electrical parts of the UMO and a pedal-operated machine for securing it in its case. Some of the jigs were pretty complex to handle, as we had to locate the UMO in them in exactly the right position.

There were eight Irish women on my line, six West Indians and me. Most of them had worked at UMEC for years and knew each other well. It was known as a friendly line, despite some major conflicts – the West Indians said it was friendly because there were so many of them. They addressed each other as 'ladies' and referred to themselves collectively as 'girls'; but the men always talked down to us as 'girls'.* The Irish women were all under thirty, except for the two who were deaf and dumb – they were in their early forties. The black women were older and most had grown-up children. Many of the women in the shop had a friend, sister or cousin working on another line, and rushed over to sit with her for ten minutes during the breaks. Everyone had known somebody already working at UMEC before they started and they thought I was very brave coming all on my own.

The co-operation between the women on our line also made it more efficient. If someone in front had forgotten to put a small clip or peg on the UMO, we would shout to them to send one along the line and attach it ourselves, or take it up to them to put right. What we were supposed to do, however, was to put out the UMO as a reject, marking down the fault both on it and on a sheet of paper. Then the reject operator would collect it, mend it, and return it to where it had left the line, also marking down the fault twice. Of course, all that took much longer.

For the first few weeks I sat with Rosemary, then I was shunted to wherever someone was missing for the next couple of months, and had to learn about fifteen different jobs.

---

* I shall refer to us/them as 'women' and use the term 'girls' only for the 16- to 18-year-olds and for reporting what the women said about themselves.

Then Rosemary was promoted to reject operator, and I took over her job permanently. While I was moving around, sometimes to as many as five different jobs a day, I was completely exhausted. I had terrible pains in my neck and back, and found it hard to keep up with the speed of the line – but the trays kept coming so I just had to carry on. All the jobs were fiddly, and I had to concentrate all the time, working with both hands which was very difficult at first, because I wasn't used to using my left hand, or to manipulating tiny nuts and screws at speed. Most days I was worked so hard that I couldn't look up at all, or had to work extra specially fast so that I would have time in between one tray and the next to unwrap a piece of chewing gum, or take a sip of tea.

Even for experienced assemblers it was a terrible strain trying to keep up with the line while learning a new job – although the others came and helped out for a few seconds if they saw you were really stuck and if they could spare the time. It took several weeks to get proficient at any one job, and the first few days were always hell. In no way was it 'unskilled' work; in fact, the firm relied on women staying a long time as they often had to use two replacement workers if one of the old hands was away.

Getting a permanent job meant I had my own bench, and could use its drawer for my tissues, cup and sandwiches; otherwise there was nowhere to put my belongings except on a corner of the bench or on the floor. When I got used to the quirks of my torque-checking machine, jig, airgun and the rest, the work became easier and I could keep up much better. It was very hot in the main assembly, around 75° F most days, even when it was below freezing outside, and very stuffy because the ventilation was so bad. There were only a few fans which made hardly any difference. I was lucky that the one for our line was just in front of me – the two lines next to us didn't have a fan at all; however, ours was pointing up to the ceiling so we couldn't get much breeze anyway. I wore only a thin T-shirt right through the winter months. If you didn't have to work so hard, you could just have fallen asleep from the hot stuffy atmosphere. The noise was constant – the lines rumbled along, the airguns had a high-pitched whirr, and the overhead conveyor system clanked round the corners. You had to raise your voice to talk to the person next to you, like in a crowded pub.

Altogether I must have learnt nearly half the jobs for the Princess and for the Maxi, and three or four for the Marina and Mini Clubman. I wasn't competent at all of these, and there were some jobs I never had a go at, although I watched how they were done. When you were learning a new job, Margaret, the 'training woman', demonstrated it once, then went away and left you to it. She only came back if the chargehand saw that you really didn't know what you were doing or assembled the components the wrong way round. In fact, it was best to learn a job from someone who had been doing it for some time. She would have discovered all the shortcuts and could show you exactly how to hold the components, how to move your fingers and which order to do the different operations, so you could cut out all unnecessary movements. The operators weren't paid for training new workers, of course. In fact, Margaret held the highest position for a woman on the shopfloor; even so she didn't earn much more than us and worked as a barmaid in the evenings and at weekends. She was Irish, in her forties and recently widowed, and she'd been at UMEC for over twenty years.

The first job at the top of the line required very flexible fingers. The basic mechanisms came in cases of twenty, and were placed on a ledge facing the operator. On the bench she had many tiny pieces of metal, of different shapes and colours, a bottle of silicone and a box of tiny wire springs. Her job was known as the 'build up' and involved fixing six or seven of these objects onto the basic mechanism. Some of them were so small and greasy that they jumped all over the place, and the wire springs became intertwined with each other and had to be prised apart. She also had to dip a nut in special grease and magnetise it in a machine before attaching it to the basic mechanism, and she finished by removing a date label from a roll of sticky labels and sticking it on the back of the basic mechanism.

I spent only a few days at this job, while Ann who did it permanently was off sick. It was nearly impossible because my fingers weren't dextrous enough; some of the components were so small they slipped out of my fingers and I couldn't get them on right. It took ages to learn the order they went in and the best way to attach them to the basic mechanism. At speed, I dropped everything or stuck the bits on the wrong way round – but you were supposed to get used to it in the end. Ann had been doing it for two years and was very quick, and she said she had been as useless as me when she started.

The 'build up' was before the light, so your pace of work wasn't regulated directly by the light flashing, and you didn't really know how many basic mechanisms to build up or at what speed. Ann just kept at it the whole time, never giving herself a rest – so she'd always done more than enough to 'feed' the light and keep the line supplied.

Ann was the only quiet person on the line. She didn't chat very much and at break sat with her friend on the next line. She did all the overtime she could, in the evenings and on Saturdays. She was single, about thirty and shared a flat with friends. The others seemed to feel a bit sorry for Ann – as if she was 'on the shelf', even though she often went dancing. She looked pale and drawn, worn out for her age, yet when she came back from Ireland after Christmas her face was shining and rosy, and most of the lines round her eyes had disappeared.

Concentrating on those tiny objects all day gave me eye strain, not helped by the glaring overhead fluorescent strip lighting. The build up was fiddly, but not as demanding physically as some of the other jobs which involved carrying boxes, lifting your arms and turning round. The others thought Ann a bit daft for building up so many basic mechanisms when she could have taken it a bit more easily. She must have been deep in daydreams, because keeping hard at it for eight hours without talking to anyone was mind-bogglingly boring.

The second job was to attach a module to the basic mechanism. On the Princess this was a big job (see Figure 3.1). You had to subassemble the components before screwing them onto the mechanism. First, two 'brakes' had to be screwed onto either side of the basic mechanism in a special jig; it was hard to locate the 'brakes' in the jig so that the screws would go in straight. Then you placed a silicone on the basic mechanism, again in a particular position, making sure that the centres of the basic mechanism and the silicone were in alignment, and put a small valve through a hole in the module. Finally, using a different jig, you attached the two components together, screwing the module together with its silicone and valve, onto the basic mechanism with its 'brakes'.

Often the screws had faulty threading, the silicones were scratched or the modules were dusty, all of which had to be rectified before starting the job; otherwise it would be rejected as 'bad work' further down the line, and have to be dismantled and reassembled. When cheaper materials were introduced, sometimes one-third of the silicones in a box of 500 were scratched and had to be thrown away, or a whole batch of screws was faulty. Inspecting them all made the job harder and wasted a lot of time. Frequently the screwing machine decided not to work properly and the chargehand and engineers had an ongoing debate about whether this was due to the screws or the machine – they never listened to the woman doing the job who knew perfectly well which was at fault. Attaching modules to the Princess involved so many different tasks that you couldn't work up any great speed at it even when you were used to the job; when new women started, the chargehand usually divided it into two separate jobs, the brakes and the modules, for two operators.

Modules were also before the light, across the conveyor from Ann and just under Eamonn's nose. You could hear all his conversations with the supervisors or progress chasers and find out which components we were low on, and how many of this set were to be done. I became quite fast at modules, but hated being at the top of the line. As Ann was so quiet there was no one to talk to, and all the others were behind me so I didn't really feel part of the line. I had to regulate my own speed and could decide to work extra hard and then have a short rest, but I didn't like that either. There was a general rule that there should be quite a large build up of trays with moduled basic mechanisms ready for the next person, the calibrator – in fact, quite a few more than she needed. The women sitting behind thought you were useless if you supplied her with only the UMO she was to send down the line next, although I couldn't see any point in building up too many. In any case, Ann gave you so many basic mechanisms that there was no space on the bench for them

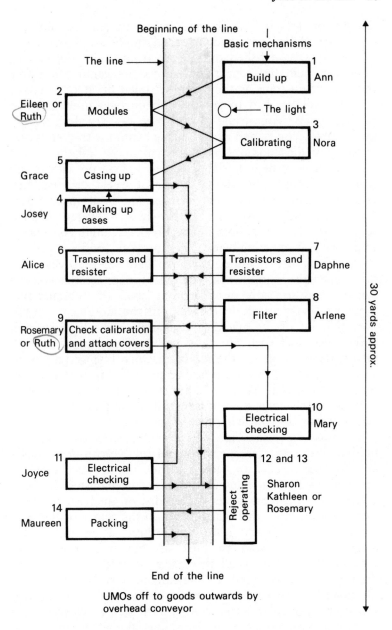

Figure 3.1 Jobs on the line: The Princess UMO

unless you attached their module pretty quickly and sent them on. When you had attached modules to two basic mechanisms, you fished out a tray from under the moving conveyor belt and sent them on to the calibrator. Often there were no trays as they were all piled up at the back of the line, so you had to get up and run right down the line to find some. You would always run, never walk, so as to save a few seconds, and avoid getting behind with your work.

Nobody did modules as a permanent job all the time I was there. Any new workers seemed to end up with it and several of them left after a couple of weeks because they couldn't stand it. The nuts, screws and basic mechanisms were black and greasy and the bench was covered in dust, so you had to spend most of the breaks cleaning your hands so as to avoid smearing black grease on your food.

Attaching the modules was also hard on the eyes, with no direct light on the work. The machine for screwing on the 'brakes' was so badly designed that you had to manoeuvre your arms very carefully to pick out the modules from the box in front of the machine. Its handle had a big red knob which was level with my eyes, and I often banged my eye into it trying to get at the modules. Once I banged my hand so hard against it that it bruised and swelled up, and Eamonn sent me to have it bandaged up in first aid. That saved me a few minutes' work so it was worth it, and lots of visitors came over to find out what had happened.

On most other sets, apart from the Princess, attaching the module was a shorter operation and the woman doing it sat at Ann's bench back to back with her. On the Maxi you had to paint two small holes in the basic mechanism with blue silicone, then place a saucer-shaped disc on the basic mechanism, followed by a dial which went on the centre of the disc, aligning pin-head-sized holes in all three. Then you used a magnetised screwhead to pick up pin-sized screws, and screwed them through all three sets of holes to secure the three components together. The silicone was dark and made the holes hard to align because you couldn't see them clearly, and there was a knack to picking up the screws which I never acquired. You could easily misjudge the entrance to the holes, knock the screws off the magnetic head, scratch the dials with the screwdriver, or put the screws in crooked. If you did any one of these you had to unscrew the whole lot with a manual screwdriver and start all over again. If you got flustered there was no time to stop and calm down before having another go – you just had to carry on as fast as you could. By the end of the day you could hardly see straight – everything was swimming around out of focus as your field of vision was concentrated on the tiny holes. I never got the hang of the job at all; Margaret said I was too heavy handed with the screwdriver to pick up the screws straight, but all new women had the same problem as me so you would think they could have used an easier machine.

The other lines in the shop had a separate operator for modules even on small sets. Ann was so fast at her build-up, though, that when we were assembling the Maxi UMO she did modules as well as her own job, working at break-neck speed. She received no sympathy from the others because each was specified as a one-person job on the layout and she was silly to accept the work of two. If there was an extra woman on the line, Eamonn would get her to help out Ann with the modules, but if it was her first attempt at the job she'd make so many rejects that Ann had to take over anyway.

After modules, the UMO was calibrated. Our calibrator was Nora, one of the deaf and dumb women. It was a tricky job and if she did it wrong there was trouble further down the line. I never had a go at calibrating but Nora showed me what she did. First, she 'roached' a box of sprockets – this seemed to mean banging their tips in a special machine. Then the basic mechanism had to be magnetised in an ancient looking box; Nora couldn't wear her watch or that would be magnetised too. Next she attached the sprocket to the basic mechanism, and calibrated it for torque. She had to match up the sprocket with the module, looking at them from left and right as well as straight on. When she'd got it exactly right from all angles, she used a foot pedal to secure the sprocket in position.

The light was by Nora and she 'fed' it, putting out a tray on the line every time it flashed. The tray scraped against a wire in a box fixed against the side of the conveyor and this registered the number of trays that went down the line. For some reason, we weren't supposed to know how many we had done, but we did check now and then to make sure we weren't doing too many.

Nora liked to have a massive build up of trays with calibrated UMOs, sometimes as many as forty, which she piled up all around her. Because of this she could give herself extra rests around the breaks. On other lines, the calibrators missed a light now and then to give the women behind a bit of a let up especially if there was a pile up of trays, but Nora never did. This would have been against the rules – the calibrator was allowed to miss a light only on the instructions of the chargehand, never the women, and as the number of UMOs for the day was laid down, they would have found out if she cheated. Towards the end of the afternoon, Nora read her paper or started taking off her overall, and still fed the next few flashes so the women behind had to carry on working after she'd stopped. This caused a lot of tension. From about 4.07 p.m. we thought every tray she put on the line would be the last one – but there were always another two or three. We wanted her to stop feeding on the dot of 4.10, so that we could also start getting ready to go home. You couldn't leave trays piled up at your position overnight as you'd never be able to keep up in the morning if you had them to do as well as those coming down the line. If the 'swing shift' – the night workers who did a 6–10 p.m. shift – were on they wouldn't do them either and were likely to leave you even more trays in return. Nora became quite anxious that we were talking about her, and kept looking round to see if we were watching her feed the light.

The younger women thought Nora was 'mad for work' because she believed that the more trays we did, the more bonus we'd get. After work and on Saturdays, she did a cleaning job at the shopping centre nearby, and she never got home before 9 p.m. So she was thought to be 'money mad' as well, and the women despised her concern to save; they thought she must be 'loaded' in any case, working all the time and hardly ever splashing out.

Grace did the fourth job, 'casing up', attaching the UMO into its first case. She had to get the cases out of large cardboard boxes, paint over a hole in them with silicone, and clip a blue circuit board for electrical fittings onto the back of the case with five small white pegs. Then she placed the plastic case with a rubber ring through its hole into the jig, slotted in the UMO and secured them all mechanically with a foot pedal, so the back of the basic mechanism stuck through the hole, cushioned by the rubber ring. Then she used another jig to fix diodes through the back of the case, and she painted over any screws that had been scratched by the module operator with black Pentel.

Grace had been casing up for nearly ten years, but often she couldn't keep up as there was much too much to do in the time. Some sets required even more subassembling on the cases, screwing on a small green plastic disc for the diode. Grace managed to have the job retimed and sub-divided but only after much fuss. Before, she was always so 'up the wall' – a long pile of trays in front of her waiting to be done and getting longer every time the light flashed – that everyone else complained as well because they weren't being fed trays at regular intervals. Those of us sitting behind shouted to Grace to 'stop chatting and send us a regular feed'. This was a joke but the job was in fact easier if your trays arrived at regular intervals; if not, you'd have none for a couple of minutes, followed by a whole rush of them which would put you 'up the wall' as well.

Grace had to work so fast that she made mistakes, so there were more rejects which made more work for us all in the long run. For a few weeks, any spare worker was sent to help Grace with the circuit board and diode, until she complained so often that they sent the time-study man to retime the whole job. Preparing the case was then made into a separate job with more subassembling, attaching two part-cases together. Whoever did it had to keep Grace supplied with cases but wasn't directly regulated by the light. It was a very boring job and Josephine, one of the young girls, got so fed up with it that she larked around and put Grace 'up the wall' by not making up enough. That cost Josey her job in the end.

Grace sat on the other side of the line from Nora, but their conversation was limited to sign language and written notes, so Grace used to turn round to chat with the two other West Indian women behind her. You could hear them laughing all the time. Grace was from Jamaica and had been at UMEC ever since her daughter Yvonne was a toddler. She lived in a block of high-rise council flats. She wanted Yvonne to be a barrister and sometimes brought me her maths homework to help with. She was enraged by Tory Party statements about immigrants, and was very upset when the homes of Anti-Nazi League supporters were bombed. It was only because there were so many West Indians that London had any transport or medical services, she said. She thought life would be much more difficult for everyone if the Tories won the general election, and that Margaret Thatcher would want to repatriate Irish people as well as West Indians.

The morning after Tory plans for immigration control were announced, Grace attacked me as soon as she arrived, saying that 'you English want to send us all home'. The only way I could get her to accept that I opposed the plans even though I was English was to emphasise that my parents had been immigrants too. Everyone on the line took part in the argument and Rosemary settled it by launching into Grace with 'Ruth's no more English than your Yvonne.' After that, the Irish referred to me as an immigrant like everyone else, and they stopped apologising when they made rude remarks about the royal family. Grace felt the British were very ungrateful for all the work West Indians had done over here and that politicians were plain ignorant in talking about restricting entry, when there had been virtually no West Indian immigrants coming over for years. If Britain threw out the blacks, Jamaica could just as well throw out all the whites 'to show our strength'. In any case, living conditions were much better back home than here. This was a recurrent topic of conversation between the four West Indian women who sat close together – everyone was healthier back home, the climate and food were better and so were the schools.

The job after 'casing up' was inserting the transistors. On the Princess it was such a large job that they had two operators for it, Alice and Daphne, who sat on opposite sides of the line and each assembled one UMO in a tray. There were three transistors – blue, red and green – which came in separate trays of twenty. They had to fix the UMO in a jig, take one transistor from each of the three trays, stick the transistors' 'legs' (each had two) through six holes in the plastic case, making sure to get all the transistors the right way round and not upside down; then they secured the case in the jig, swivelled the jig over so the case was held in upside down, put six washers over each of the transistors' legs and over the circuit board (and these often jumped off as they were so small and light), took six nuts and screwed these down onto the washers and the legs with the airgun. Then they had to take three metal clips, locate them in another different three holes in the case, take three screws and screw down the clips using a second airgun with a different fitting. Then a resistor had to be pushed deep into the holes to make contact with the clips, and this required a special hand tool. It was easy to screw down the nuts and screws sideways so they wouldn't go in properly, and then the whole thing had to be put out as a reject.

Alice and Daphne had to complete all of this within two minutes. They were hampered by boxes – each had three trays of transistors and three larger boxes that the trays came in, also boxes of resisters as well as the large jig and all the other bits and pieces. The bench was so crowded that they were in danger of knocking the components onto the floor and had to stack the trays of transistors by the side of the line. However, this was no solution as they got in the way of the trays travelling along the line which then got stuck across the line.

Alice was in her late fifties but looked much younger. She was tall and slim, her hair was dyed black and straightened, and she often wore a brown bobble hat. Her husband had recently retired from London Transport, and they had four grown-up children, one of whom still lived at home. Alice was kind and warm, and very affectionate towards me from the beginning. The second week I was there she put her arms round me while we were standing at the union meeting, and took my hand in hers. She was always calling me 'honey-bunch' and 'little one', and took hold of my arm or hand if we were walking in the same direction. I reminded her of her eldest grandchild, who was supposed to be bigger than I was even though she was only eleven.

Alice was very religious, and kept a prayer book in her bench drawer, which she would read after the *Mirror* and *Sun*, when the line was stopped. She was a fervent church-goer, and wished that the annual holidays were in June instead of July so she could go home to the annual church convention in Jamaica. She and her husband were planning to go home for good when they could afford to. Alice often sang hymns to herself, and called us 'sister', but she wasn't a Bible basher. To me she seemed the epitome of 'God-fearing' – she bore no malice towards anyone. Alice didn't drink, smoke, or approve of gambling, as she told me when I asked which horse she was backing in our line's sweepstake for the Grand National. One day there was a lot of fuss about exactly when we were allowed to line up at the clock to go home. When the supervisors indulged their petty authority, I was taken aback to hear Alice mutter that the supervisor 'wasn't fit to be alive'; although we all agreed with her it was strange hearing it come from Alice. She often came out with parables and sayings which I found hard to grasp at first, partly because her accent was much stronger than the other West Indians', but she didn't mind repeating them for me.

Her husband was rather bored since he had retired. He spent the day reading, tending his vegetable patch, and then he prepared dinner for them both. It was clear that most husbands did the shopping and cooking if they were at home. Sometimes Alice ran up the High Street at lunchtime to shop, or put money in the bank, as this was the only time we could get to the bank while it was open. When I went too, we ran hand in hand the quarter mile up to the National Westminster, and back again as quickly as possible to have time to eat our lunch. Alice came to work by bus and always told me if she had seen me on my bike from the top of the bus. She, Rosemary and I took turns during the day to fill our flasks with hot water from an ancient machine to make our tea with.

On principle, Alice never complained to the chargehand about the transistors job, nor about another on a different set that was simply impossible to do in the time. From experience she had learnt that if you asked to have the job retimed yourself, you could land up with more work, or even be taken 'upstairs' for a warning as you were admitting you had difficulty keeping up. Two lines away an elderly English woman had trouble keeping up, and as she was slowing down the line, the others said that management was trying to ease her out or reduce her bonus. So Alice kept quiet and just carried on working through the breaks if she was 'up the wall'. She supported the dispute, but trusted in divine justice rather than the union to sort out the factory and give the supervisors their just deserts.

Daphne was from Grenada, and was much younger and more worldly than Alice. She wore steel-rimmed glasses and had an Afro hairstyle. She looked very young, but had two children working already, the girl in an office and the boy as an apprentice. Her husband worked in a light-bulb factory. Daphne was very sharp and inquisitive; she had to know everything about you, and made personal comments all the time. Even so, she wouldn't answer any question put to her, always replying 'never you mind' to everything said to her. Every morning she wanted to know whether I had come by bike, why I was or wasn't wearing a scarf. She asked everyone who walked past her bench where they were going, counted how many cups of tea we drank during the day and how often we went to the loo. Rosemary said Daphne had ears on the line, as she knew what everyone behind her was talking about without turning round, and repeated it all to Grace and Alice. Boredom must have been the reason for Daphne's obsession with everything that happened on the shopfloor. She created some interest in the place for herself by calling out to everyone who went past, but it exasperated the chargehands because she called them over even when she hadn't run out of components or broken down.

After a few weeks I could hardly move without a comment from Daphne and Rosemary encouraged me to take a stand against her. All three black women had me fetching them cups of soup, sandwiches, even fish and chips from the canteen at lunchtime, and Rosemary said if I was soft, of course they would take me for a ride. So I refused to do any more errands for a while, and said 'never you mind' to all

Daphne's comments and questions, which solved the problem.

Like Alice, Daphne was also religious but in a more sophisticated way. She had a 'Jesus loves you' sticker on her bag but I don't doubt she thought God would strike down the supervisors for their evil deeds. She was also much more sensitive than appeared at first sight. When I asked how long she'd lived here, she 'never you mind' and wouldn't answer me at all, except to say that her children were born here. It turned out she thought I was accusing her of having a very strong accent and not speaking English properly, which hadn't entered my head. I told her I found some of the Irish accents much harder to understand, and that my own parents had much stronger accents than her despite having lived here longer. It took some time to realise that they thought of me as being the only one who spoke 'proper English', a rather double-edged compliment.

Back to the line – on smaller sets like the Maxi (see Figure 3.2), Daphne did the transistors on her own and Alice sat three places further down the line with Arlene, just behind me. After the transistors, the jobs were different on the different sets. On the Princess the filter was assembled and attached; then came torque checking and covers for the basic mechanism, transistors and filter; the next job was checking of all the electrical parts of the UMO which took two operators; the last job was packing.

On the Maxi, after Daphne put in the transistors, the sixth woman on the line, Rosemary or me, checked the torque and attached the resister; the seventh put three metal clips on the side edges of the case to attach the UMO into the vehicle; the next job took two operators who made up nickel-plated covers to fit over the basic mechanism and transistors, and the tenth operator attached these covers as well as diodes; then came electrical checking and finally packing.

The filter job on the Princess was another that was virtually impossible to complete in the time, and Arlene was always 'up the wall'. If she was away, they had two or even three women doing it. Eventually it was simplified and the filters arrived already assembled so Arlene had less screwing

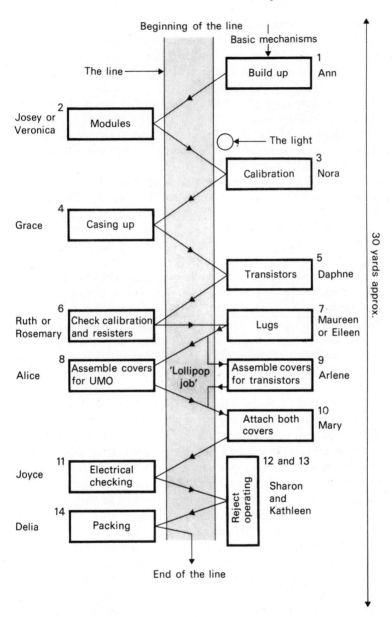

Figure 3.2 Jobs on the line: The Maxi UMO

to do. I really noticed the difference because the trays came to me at much more regular intervals and made my job easier. Before, Arlene had built up nine or ten at a go, letting her trays pile up on the line in front of her; then she attached all the filters to the UMOs, saving a few movements and therefore a few seconds. The filters came packaged in poly-styrene moulds, in small cardboard boxes, inside larger boxes, and Arlene had to unpack all three before starting to assemble them and find somewhere to throw the empties. She too was surrounded by boxes.

The job I ended up with entailed checking the calibration, putting out rejects and some assembly. First I had to fix the UMO onto the torque-checking machine, a hot, noisy metal thing, and check that the calibration was correct. Then I checked that the rotors on the basic mechanism were properly aligned and moved round freely. I had to see that the pin which the sprocket touched was straight, and then turn over the UMO to check the circuit board, nuts, screws and diodes on the back. Some had been calibrated wrongly, or the spro-cket didn't move freely, or the rotors were caught, or the pin was bent. I had to mark down the fault on the UMO for the reject operator, and on a quality control form, and take the UMO off the line. There were several rejects every hour, and many more if the line was running fast.

Then there was assembling to be done. On the Princess I cleaned the dusty transistors, slotted a diactor over them, and attached two aluminium covers, a double one which fitted over the basic mechanism and transistors, and a single one for the filter. This one had a centre hole through which I had to fit a small valve. The covers came in skips of 1,000; I reloaded them into smaller boxes of twenty so they would fit onto the bench. These ran out within half an hour so it felt as if I was constantly jumping up to change over heavy boxes, pile up empty ones and fetch more cases of diactors. The covers were wrapped in polythene bags which had to be removed and I needed a rubbish box for these and a separate one for reject diactors and aluminium covers. I used a radio-active spray to remove dust from the transistors and the covers, holding the spray in my right hand and balancing it on my lap while I did the other operations. I had to wear gloves to avoid getting oil smudges on the inside of the covers, but as these were made of cotton and were fluffy, it was a losing battle against oil and fluff. Every time I reloaded the boxes with covers and sat down, I had to rearrange the spray, gloves and diactors.

If I sent on a UMO with dust or oil smudges, Mary, the electrical checker who sat behind me, would come and tell me off. She was the other deaf and dumb woman, and as there was a long distance between her and me along the line, I had to perch the tray very carefully on the conveyor belt to get it to travel straight. If it got stuck against the sides of the conveyor she banged her wooden stick behind me very loud so that I would turn round and see, and run down the line to put it right. All in all, there was quite a lot to do in the one minute allowed for each UMO. It was impossible to keep up unless the trays came at regular two-minute intervals, and difficult even then.

On the Maxi, after torque checking, I attached three metal clips, three screws and the resister. This job was excruciating at first; by 10 a.m. my neck and back were in agony from straining forward to press on the airgun and I didn't know how I would get through the day. I often put the clips in wrong, as two went one way round while the third went the opposite way, and I was slow with the screws. You had to hold the three screws in your left hand, and the airgun in your right, twiddle the screws onto the magnetic head of the gun, and then screw them down. Obviously it was quicker if you had the next screw ready in your left hand and didn't have to put down the airgun in between each. My left hand was so inflexible for the first few weeks that I had to do it all with my right hand which took at least six times as long, but otherwise I would never have managed to get the screws in at all. I should say that I'm not particularly clumsy or bad with my hands, but these jobs required an expertise that could come only with much practice. After several weeks solid, I could do the job without it hurting and I became so fast at it that I could talk to the person next to me, or even let a couple of trays pile up while I rushed to the coffee machine, because I knew I'd be able to get 'down the wall' quick enough.

Whenever I could finally do a job, it became very very

boring. You had to look at it and concentrate all the time, so your mind had to be on the work. After a few hours, you hoped for a breakdown or for someone to run out of components. Usually we changed sets every day, but occasionally we stayed on the same set for two whole days and that was really terrible. Then you longed for a changeover even to a harder set. As it happened, many changeovers were 'to the same thing', the same set but with a different module or diactor.

Margaret kept telling me that the torque checker could save a lot of work further down the line if she did her job well. This was true – you could see most of the faults but there was never time enough for a close inspection nor to do the job properly. When you put out a reject, the reject operator returned it to you mended half an hour or so later. Then you had to do the assembly work on it and recheck it, find a spare tray and feed it into the line spaced in between the other trays so Mary wouldn't get 'up the wall'. As trays were coming down the line towards you as normal, dealing with the returned rejects was really extra work which you had to fit in somehow. It was in my interests not to put out all the rejects but just send them on as if I hadn't noticed the faults and let the electrical checker find them, saving myself a little effort and time. Sometimes when I was very hard pressed, I'd ignore dust or oil smudges but never faulty calibration which was much more serious and I would have been caught out soon enough. It didn't take long to realise that the more conscientious I was, the more work I created for myself.

On our line all this was complicated by the conflict between the electrical checker and the reject operator. Sharon, the reject operator, was only young but she was very bossy and told tall stories about how much she'd won at bingo, how much land she owned and how much her rings were worth; no one believed a word she said. She also stirred up trouble by telling tales on us to Eamonn and interfered in our work. She sat opposite Joyce, the West Indian electrical checker, who was a very determined person and wouldn't let anyone put her down or out-talk her. They chattered all day about the price of this and that, but they hated each other's guts. Sharon tried to cut down on her own work and kept saying the UMOs I put out for her weren't faulty. She wanted me to send them down the line 'to see if Joyce puts them out'. If the torque registered wrong on my machine, she insisted it was all right on hers, or if the sprocket was catching she banged the UMO hard down on the bench till it moved. It got to the stage where she wouldn't take any reject of mine for a mechanical fault unless I had already banged it and rechecked it – this meant twice as much work for me and none for her. If I sent UMOs down the line with dirty modules or bent pins, Joyce would come and bawl me out so I was really caught between the two of them. To stop Sharon I put on a show of calling over Eamonn and asked whether or not it was my job to put out rejects as there was no point even checking them if they were just replaced on the line without being mended. This put an end to it for a few days, but I had to keep 'giving out' to Sharon and threaten to have the calibrating machine and the two torque-checking machines checked so we'd see if they really were different.

On the Maxi, someone sat across the line from me to do the 'lugs'. At first this was Eileen who finally left at Christ-mas to go back to Cork for good. Once I could cope with the resisters we used to chat all day. She told me about her school and how the teachers made her feel so stupid that she gave up answering questions even when she knew the right answers, and then they thought she was even more stupid. This was a common complaint amongst the younger ones – especially if they'd gone to school in London: the teachers didn't care about them and hadn't taught them anything, so they weren't going to bother with day release now. Eileen was enormous and pasty looking, living, it seemed, on Crun-chie bars and bags of sweets. Grace and Arlene were forever going on about her eating habits and coaxed her to eat a proper cooked meal in the canteen; they said she could eat a Crunchie bar afterwards if she liked.

Josey did the lugs on and off for a couple of months after Christmas until she got the sack. Then her friend Maureen took over. She was only 19 but looked much older; she had come from Waterford the year before. At home she had lived in as a domestic in a pub; then she worked at the local Wool-worth before coming to UMEC. She was lively too, like Josey, and spent the day interpreting dreams, having her fortune told, and telling jokes about nuns and the devil. She was anti-church and went round with a gang of girls that drank and swore, disapproved of by most of the other Irish women. She was engaged and turned out to be very pregnant though it hardly showed, and she left to have twins. She was living with her boyfriend but couldn't see any point in getting married – 'I can't have a white wedding while I look like this!' Basically she was homeless because her landlord would evict her if he discovered a man there, let alone babies. Maureen had no money and didn't know about maternity benefit or social security till I got the forms for her. She wasn't going to tell her parents till the baby was born because she said they lived in the country and were very narrow minded; they'd be so shocked they might disown her. I didn't think she had much to look forward to but she wasn't worried. Like the other young ones, she was only at UMEC for the money and was glad of a good excuse to leave.

Alice and Arlene sat directly behind Maureen and me to do the Maxi covers. These had to be subassembled on the line unlike my covers for the Princess which came ready to attach. The machinery, components and covers were very old-fashioned in comparison with the Princess – nickel, cardboard, and paper bags instead of aluminium and polythene bags. Making the covers was known as the 'lollipop job' because all the components were round and flat like a big lollipop. Alice and Arlene were supplied with round pieces of nickel, cardboard rings called 'bezzels', round metal rings to fit round the edge of the nickel and a thick black ring of plastic for them all to be placed in. They cleaned the nickel, both by hand with their cotton gloves and with an airspray. Then they fixed the bezzel into the metal ring, placed the plastic ring upside down in the jig, the nickel on top of it, followed by the metal ring and bezzel. They had to slot these together exactly right so the handles of the jig could be rotated to secure them all together to make one piece. This was the cover and was sent down the line to Mary.

Altogether Maxi covers required three operators – Arlene made up covers for the transistors, Alice for the basic mechanism and Mary attached them both to the UMO. The lollipop job was the easiest on the line; even so, you could push the handle too hard and crack the nickel and it took considerable skill to slot all the pieces in the jig so they wouldn't fall apart again when you took out the cover. After a couple of hours it was very boring but I didn't mind being put on covers because I knew I wouldn't get tired out.

Behind Mary, Joyce did electrical checking. It was hard on her eyes but not too physically demanding. Joyce stood two assembled UMOs on special stands, attached leads to all their electrical fittings and inspected whether they all functioned as they should. If they passed the test, she stuck code and date labels on the back; if not, she put them out as rejects.

The last job was packing. Everyone else seemed to hate it because you had to stand up. Maureen, Josey and Rosemary always moaned when they were put on packing but I quite liked it as you had a bit more freedom of movement. It was heavy work, folding very stiff sheets of cardboard round the UMO to make a protective box. The cardboard scratched your arms and wrists. You found a skip, lifted it onto a stand, put twelve boxes in it, then lifted it onto the moving overhead conveyor. You had to stamp labels for the skip and remember to stick them on each new skip. In the spare seconds between the boxes, you were supposed to assemble diodes for use further up the line, pushing the diode into a holder – most of us refused as we had no seconds to spare. One packer on another line was said to take home the diodes and holders and make up 3,000 every evening so there wouldn't be so much pressure on her at work. After packing all day your arms and legs ached, but at least you could move around a little; your movements weren't so directly regulated by the line as there was no one behind waiting for a tray from you. Once you got the hang of the cardboard shapes and could keep up with the speed, you could pack a whole batch and then take a short rest or even walk around a few steps.

The reject operators sat at the back facing the line. Some of the time they were very busy but quite often they had little to do and sat chatting. Apart from Sharon, there was Kathleen who had been at UMEC for thirteen years though she looked only about thirty. She was very quiet probably because Sharon talked non-stop, and she hummed Irish folk songs. Kathleen was a chainsmoker and addicted to Coca Cola, a can nearly always in her hand. Apart from mending the rejects, they had to replace women who were away, and 'relieve' whoever wanted to go to the loo, so they had to know all the jobs on the line. In the morning they took orders from the rest of us for the canteen and brought back rolls, hard-boiled eggs and orange juice in time for the first break. When we were doing a small set like the Maxi, we had no proper breaks when the whole line stopped except at 9.50 a.m. and 2.30 p.m. For our other 'unofficial' breaks at 9.10, 11.10 and 3.10, Kathleen and Sharon 'relieved' each of us in turn for ten minutes. We all hated being 'on relief' because it didn't give us a proper rest; there was nowhere to sit because Kathleen or Sharon was on your chair and no one to talk to as everyone else was working. It was just a way of keeping the line running continuously.

Reject operating was a higher status than the rest because you had to know all the jobs. It was paid a grand 2p more an hour which made little difference to the pay packet at the end of the week. Rosemary hesitated for a long time when Eamonn asked her if she wanted to be a reject operator – she preferred being part of the line; many reject operators were unpopular with the other women who thought they had an easy life.

A tray took about twenty minutes to travel from the beginning of the line to the end. During that time, fifteen of us transformed two small basic mechanisms into complete UMOs ready to be put in a vehicle. The pressure to churn out hundreds of them was constant; it ensured a high level of production for the firm but it certainly took its toll on us. At the end of the day we were all 'jaded', but which limbs ached most depended on the particular job you'd been doing. The 'build up', modules, calibrating and all the checking jobs were hard on the eyes – concentrating so hard all the time and focusing on small holes and objects made your head buzz. Casing up, transistors, covers and packing were heavy work; in the one minute allowed for each UMO you were moving all the time – lifting boxes, changing over trays, throwing away bags and cases as well as doing the actual assembling. Unless you were well organised and knew exactly in which order to do the different movements, the work would get on top of you and you'd be up the wall with no chance of stopping to sort yourself out. But however well you were organised and could keep up with the line, the speed and the amount of work tired you out. The jobs between calibrating and electrical checking were the central ones, controlled by the light; you felt part of a chain and had more contact with the other women. It was like being one large collective worker. Although we were more dominated by the light than the jobs at the front and back of the line we could also enjoy breakdowns more fully. We had nothing 'to be getting on with', like building up more basic mechanisms or assembling diodes, so if the line stopped we had a rest.

Differences between the jobs were minor in comparison with the speed and discipline which the line imposed on us all. We couldn't do the things you would normally not think twice about, like blowing your nose or flicking hair out of your eyes; that cost valuable seconds – it wasn't included in the layout so no time was allowed for it. In any case, your hands were usually full. We all found the repetition hard to take; once you were in command of your job, repeating the same operations over and over thousands of times a day made you even more aware of being controlled by the line. You couldn't take a break or swap with someone else for a change – you just had to carry on; resisting the light or the speed only made the work harder because the trays kept coming and eventually you would have to work your way through the pile-up. If you really couldn't keep up with the line, you were out.

Chapter Four
Getting to know the women

Arlene

Arlene was a Jamaican woman in her late forties, who lived with her two grown-up daughters of twenty and twenty-two. She had come to England in the mid-1950s and had worked at UMEC for over ten years, doing the same job on our line for several years. As I often worked directly behind her on the other side of the line, we were in close contact. She was always glamorously dressed in lurex jumpers, short skirts and very high heels, and wore a bouffant-style wig, though for months I thought her hair was straightened and dyed light brown. She used lipstick and powder to make her skin lighter, and was generally concerned with her appearance. She complained that men were always stopping her in the street and propositioning her, but I suspect she was quite flattered by their attention. She said she kept in tune with 'the younger generation's' music and fashions through her daughters. Both of them were clerical workers. The older one was at the Gas Board and sang in her free time; she had been on television and made a record. The younger one worked for the DHSS and was doing an Open University course. Arlene was on good terms with them, more like an equal than a mother, and they shared the cooking and housework. The elder daughter's German boyfriend was also living with them temporarily.

Arlene's ideas about life were very definite. She was really clued up about British and American colonialism in the Caribbean, and the position of black people and women generally, as well as UMEC's tactics towards the workforce.

She also believed in God, spirits, and folklore, and her under-standing of all events in the factory was filtered through these beliefs. She was very philosophical, happy to sit think-ing all day, and would ponder over what we were discuss-ing, often bringing it up again several days later. She liked reading although she didn't have much time for it, and was working her way page by page through an encyclopedia at home.

We had long discussions about what we both meant by 'class', all the different ways you could define it, and what different classes there were in Britain and Jamaica. She thought a person's class depended on their behaviour and personality, and wouldn't agree that economic position had anything to do with it. We also discussed such things as the family structure in the different ethnic groupings, what we meant by 'boredom', and whether or not 'intelligence' really exists. We also had an ongoing debate about what happens to our bodies after we die, as she thought 'we are too good just to go under the ground'. I can't hope to put over the quality of these discussions, but Arlene would hold her own in any abstract philosophical debate.

Arlene had an elaborate set of ideas about how the body works and what food is good for different organs. Gin flushes out the womb and so is a woman's drink. Hot flushes clear out the system, and whisky is good for cleaning out the brain now and then. She said she could tell from our looks whether we had eaten meat the night before. One morning she told me that a spirit had come in through her window during the night and pinned her to her bed so she couldn't move at all. She said spirits could inhabit you, and give you power to destroy your enemies. If she went home with some-one in her mind, it was a bad sign for them as all sorts of dis-asters would befall them. She even held herself responsible for the previous supervisor having dropped down dead, as she had gone home with him in her thoughts the night before he died. Daphne, with her 'ears on the line', used to come up and tell me not to listen to all these 'crazy ideas' and insulted Arlene by saying to the others that she 'lived in a different world'. I could see there was no point starting an argument about the existence of spirits.

Arlene's beliefs about divine justice were as straight-forward as Alice's. She didn't go to church regularly or harp on about Jesus, but she knew that the Lord was on the side of the good, and would punish wrongdoers. She had such confidence in God that although she took part in the go slow when we were in dispute, she didn't think we needed to bother too much, as He would sort out the wages and get us what we were due. Past experience had proved that God helped the needy: when she was very poor and had little food for her daughters, she had put some meat and potatoes in a pot to cook, and when she went back to stir them, she found there were ten potatoes instead of two. The Lord had provided for her, though she would rather have had more meat than potatoes. On another occasion, God arranged for an Income Tax rebate just when she was low on cash, so she didn't need to worry about being poor when she was old because God helps those in need, and anyway she had a lucky streak. God also had divine control over the pools. She truly believed that the poor and meek would 'inherit the Kingdom of Heaven' and in this world too.

Any coincidence, like saying the same thing at the same time, or having seen the same film at the weekend, was evidence to Arlene of a mystical connection between us. One very long morning I asked how she stood the boredom of the job, and she said she had just been thinking exactly the same thing, so I must be psychic. I said that we had both thought of it because it really was a very boring day, but she wouldn't agree. After that she kept saying that people like her and me with special powers of telepathy should make good use of them.

Arlene was also expert at dream interpretation, and knew all the signs of good luck and bad luck. If she dreamt of a number, say 64, that meant she would die when she was sixty-four. Just before I left, I told her I'd dreamt about the factory; in the dream Sharon who brought us rolls from the canteen was making me a salad with ham, tomatoes and cucumber and asked if I wanted pieces 'from all three parts of the cucumber'. Quick as a flash, Arlene wanted to know if I had eaten the food in the dream, and heaved a sigh of relief when I said no, as that would have been a very bad sign. It was good to dream of food but not to eat it. The cucumber, she said, represented the three phases of my work life – past, present and future – and slicing it indicated there would be some 'strictness'. She also told me I was very silly to avoid walking under a particular bridge where there were lots of pigeons, as bird droppings on your head brought very good luck.

I didn't know how to respond to all these 'unscientific' beliefs, because she was absolutely convinced of them, and no amount of bringing factual evidence to the contrary made any difference. In the end I just listened and nodded. To me it was amazing that the same daily events in the factory could be understood so differently by two people. Neither of us was in the slightest doubt that her own interpretations were correct. Yet, perhaps I shouldn't have been surprised that someone like Arlene, who had so little control over the course of her own life, should trust so strongly in fate.

Arlene's favourite way of spending the evening was to sit by the fire with a bottle of rum, letting her memories surface. She had gone over and over the events in her early life and they had become a kind of personal folklore, each with particular significance. She was writing down part of her autobiography in an exercise book and wanted to do it more systematically as a book. We discussed whether it would be easier to tape herself saying it, and whether she should use the first or third person. She was worried that the events were so fantastic that no reader would believe them if she used the first person. As well as covering her own life, she wanted to include some of her strongly held views, for instance that all people over fifty are basically evil, due to their experience of wars and politics, while the young are still good.

Even on the line she mused about her past to help her keep going. For several weeks she went deaf in one ear but wouldn't go to the doctor. In the end, she admitted that she would rather sit and think than chatter to some of the other women who weren't on the same wavelength; being deaf gave her peace and quiet to think, she was grateful to the Lord for this opportunity to let the past come up into her mind. In any case, when she first came to this country, it was so noisy that she couldn't stand the din; being deaf reminded her of home.

Arlene thought that all we could hope for was a happy home life. If she had her house, her bottle of rum, the fire, and if her daughters were happy, she would be quite satisfied. 'My house is not grand, but to me it is a little palace.'

Arlene had a deep distrust of men as unreliable, childish and weak. She thought she was better off without a permanent one, since her husband had left. They only stifle you, she said, especially if they are only interested in sex, and it wasn't a good idea to settle down with just one person. She had many men friends, and could have had her pick, but she was careful not to get too close to any of them. She told horror stories of mean husbands who wouldn't fork out housekeeping money, beat their wives and literally drove them mad. A bad family situation could easily send a woman mad: 'it was enough to send her to Walton [a local mental hospital]' she said about a particularly bad husband, and thought it was only because she talked to the wife regularly to let her get her troubles off her chest that she hadn't been certified. 'Nerve trouble' in general was due to the stresses of home and work.

Arlene's family had a small farm in Jamaica and she grew up in the country. Her father had left for Cuba when she was very small and she had never seen him again. She was the darkest in her family with 'wild and woolly' hair, and her mother was evil to her because of this, accusing her of being a 'throwback'. She was convinced her mother had hated her from birth, as she had been left to die as a tiny baby, and was only discovered by chance by one of her aunties, barely alive. As a child she had worms, and was hungry all the time; her mother wouldn't feed her and called her 'mouth', so she had to go grubbing in the bush for food and eat clumps of grass. To this day, her jaw muscles are very tense, and she said she had never been able to relax her mouth since her mother made fun of her. She still hated her mother, now seventy-five. When Arlene went home to visit for the first time in twenty years a couple of years ago, her mother exclaimed that she was still as ugly as ever, and was completely uninterested

in Arlene's daughters. Arlene suspected her mother was trying to do her out of her share in the smallholding. Her
mother's hostility was to do with Arlene's darker colour. In
those days, the lighter your skin, the better you were, and
Arlene was still proud that she and her sisters had been taken
out by rich white boys in Jamaica.

Her description of the farm was idyllic. They grew red
peppers, avocados and all sorts of fruit. The air was clear
and pure, the sky blue and cloudless, the sea was calm and
warm. When you breathed, the air was so pure it really
filled your lungs. Arlene thought people at home were much
healthier than here, aged more slowly and had better complexions. On the other hand, she wouldn't want to live in
Jamaica now because she would turn into an alcoholic as
the rum was so cheap, and you could just laze around in the
sun. 'I'd be dead within six months.' Having lived here so
long now, she thought she would be irritated with how slow
everyone is and how long they take to serve you in the shops
and bars, so that after a time the relaxed atmosphere would
become boring.

Aluminium and bauxite are extracted near her mother's
house now, and the air is full of red dust. They have no
electricity at home and still depend on kerosene lamps, but
less than a mile away they can see the brightly lit alumina
works with their own generators. She explained to me the
different phases of emigration from Jamaica – first to Britain,
and then to America and Canada – and how well people have
fared in the different places. She was annoyed at the extraction of raw materials from Jamaica by foreign firms, British
in the past but now increasingly American. On the other
hand, she said 'it's their fault if they want to work so hard' –
the Jamaicans could survive without factories or industry.

As a young girl, Arlene worked in a British-owned tobacco
factory, taking leaves off the 'bones' (stalks). They were paid
2d. a pound weight for the leaves, but as they were so light
you had to have them piled up from floor to ceiling to earn
anything at all. The leaves had already been dried, and the
Jamaican growers were paid 1½d. a pound. She made only
1s. a day, and one week ate such wonderful dinners cooked
by a woman just outside the factory for a shilling each that

she spent her whole week's wages on her dinners, and had none left to take home. That was the end of that job. These tobacco leaves were used to make the very best cigars which sold for over £1 each, and the bones were used for pipe tobacco. Her aunty hand-rolled cigarettes in another factory for a similar pittance. The British owner made 'a heap of money' by exploiting the farmers and the factory workers, but again you had to give him credit for conning them so thoroughly. Alice and Grace overheard all this, and it set them off on their own experiences in tobacco factories, which led to a general discussion between all the West Indian women on Britain's 'terrible mistake in joining the Common Market', and the rise in the price of sugar by way of retaliation by the Jamaican government.

When she was in her early twenties, Arlene had come all on her own by ship to Liverpool. Her boyfriend met her at Paddington station, but he had acquired another girlfriend, and they didn't settle down together until she was pregnant some years later. She had worked throughout her time in this country, and her children were cared for by child minders when they were small so she could carry on. She never told me when her husband had left and moved to the USA, but they still correspond and he comes to visit. Arlene took great pride in her children's appearance, wanting them to be the cleanest and best dressed in the class, and she dressed them and put bows in their hair whenever she took them out, even to the doctor. She laughed that now they hand down their cast-off jeans and dresses to her. She had kept them both at school until they were eighteen despite financial hardship, but now all three were working, so they were better off.

Arlene's husband was Alice's brother, so they were sisters-in-law. Arlene said Alice was evil and had interfered in the marriage, and now tries to stop Arlene seeing her husband when he comes to England. This is Arlene's story, but I couldn't imagine Alice having bad intentions towards a fly. Arlene said she will sit and chat, but deep down she knows Alice is one of her worst enemies. Her sins towards Arlene were being repaid by misfortune, as her son's marriage had broken up and her husband had retired.

Arlene talked very openly to whites. The only overt complaint she made about racism was to do with the Notting Hill riots. At the time she was working at Oxford Circus; one evening it took her four hours to get home because white people including the bus conductor kept trying to push her off the bus, and hurled abuse at her. In the end she had to walk all the way. She said she had always got on well with 'the natives', so much so that her own people were jealous, and she felt quite split between the two groups, at times so split 'that I'm in danger of going to Walton'.

She told me about her overnight stay in New York as an example of how well she got on with people. On her way to Jamaica, she missed the plane in New York and settled down in a hotel with a bottle of duty-free vodka. When the cleaning woman came to do out the room, Arlene offered her a drink. After much persuading the woman eventually accepted and they started chatting. They got on so well that the woman invited Arlene back to her apartment in Brooklyn and they had a great party with all the neighbours. The woman also turned out to know Arlene's only brother who lived quite near. Arlene would have been quite happy to spend the whole holiday there, and now had a friend to visit in New York.

Arlene talked to me about the Irish and what she imagined their home life to be like as if I was West Indian. She said I had some black blood in me, and was probably a 'throwback' as I have curly hair and darker skin than most of the Irish women. She insisted there were lots of black people who were whiter than me.

Rosemary

Rosemary was my special friend. She was very kind to me at the beginning, made me feel at home and answered all my questions once we'd got used to each other's accents. She introduced me to everyone 'this is Ruth – it's an Irish name but she's not Irish'. She told me who was who, what sorts of things to complain about, and where everything was.

Rosemary was twenty-three, plump with a fresh freckly

face and short wavy brown hair. She wore glasses for work, because her eyes had gone bad since she worked at UMEC, and she had a strong Irish accent. She came from a large family who lived in the country about twenty miles from Dublin. She had been working since she was fifteen, for four years at Plesseys before coming over, then in Liptons supermarket, and she had been at UMEC for nearly three years. She was saving to get married and thought she would stay in the factory for at least another couple of years until they could afford to have a baby. As well as UMEC she did a part-time cleaning job straight after work from 4.30–6.15 p.m., five nights a week which brought in another £10, and she said she wouldn't be able to manage at all without this. So every afternoon she rushed off from the factory at 4.15 to get to her 'part-time' and didn't get home until 7 p.m., so she was out at work for twelve hours a day. No wonder she was exhausted. She complained the whole time of being 'jaded' and worn out, of colds, bad chests and sore eyes. She had to fit all her chores into the weekend, and when she had a busy weekend visiting friends as well as shopping and cleaning, she really did look a wreck on Monday morning, which was a bad way to start the week. But like all the women, after a few days off work, she looked completely different, esepcially round the eyes.

Rosemary shared a bedsit with Doreen, her friend from Dublin, who worked on the Mini line next to us. They paid £12 a week rent for a tiny room with a threadbare carpet, next to no furniture, and a small double bed which they shared. Electricity and gas were on meters on top of the rent. The landlord owned two adjacent houses, renting out twelve rooms like this; they thought he didn't declare his rent to the income tax, so he must have been making a packet out of them. He tried to evict Rosemary and Doreen; he hadn't paid the electricity bill although they had fed the meter, and there were no lights. They refused to pay their rent until he had the electricity reconnected. Rosemary, sticking up for herself in typical fashion, went to the Citizens Advice Bureau who sent her to the rent tribunal, and got them to threaten him with legal proceedings. However, they still looked for another flat because the landlord said he would just throw their belongings out onto the street, which they thought he was quite capable of doing.

I was taken aback when I went round to their room. It was very small, and they could only wash in the sink. They had no privacy whatsoever, and neither could ever be on her own; Rosemary couldn't see her fiancé without Doreen being there too. Their life was highly organised. On Thursdays Doreen went to Sainsbury's to do their weekly shop, and during the week she cooked their meal every night, ready for when Rosemary got back from her 'part-time'. Doreen was quite happy to do this, and was much more happy go lucky with money. She wasn't trying to save, and would rather run out during the week than have another job as well. She was older than Rosemary, twenty-seven, and went out dancing and to pubs more than Rosemary, although she didn't have a regular boyfriend. In the evenings, Rosemary just had time to have a wash and eat before Kevin, her fiancé, came round at 7.45, then they would either go round to his place or stay at hers. On Friday and Saturday evenings they usually went to the pictures, and he took her out for a meal after they had been shopping on Saturday and after Mass on Sunday.

Sunday was the only day they had time to visit friends or Kevin's three brothers and family who all lived in London, too. All four brothers were unskilled labourers – 'in the building' as Rosemary put it. Sometimes they went dancing in one of the local Irish dance halls, but never to the pub as Rosemary didn't drink, and Kevin hardly ever did. He was twenty-four, and they had met over here, but had each visited the other's family at home on holidays in Ireland. She said they would like to go home after they were married, but they would most likely stay here for another few years yet.

Kevin and Rosemary bought each other very expensive presents, mostly jewelry, like gold watches, crosses and rings and he bought her an elaborate gold and diamond engagement ring. Many of the Irish women had engagement rings and when a new one appeared everyone went to admire it. Rosemary wore her gold watch and engagement ring to work, saying 'that's what they're for, to be worn', and so she looked quite affluent although she certainly wasn't. In fact, they couldn't afford to go home in the summer, and she was going to work through the holidays, so they could save to get married. It was a choice between a holiday this year and not getting married for two years, or no holiday and perhaps getting married at the end of the year. They were looking for a flat, and that, too, would partly determine the date. In any case, Rosemary didn't want children until she was at least twenty-six or twenty-seven, and then only two, or three at the very most. She thought she would go back to work when they went to school, but would stay at home with them till then. 'What's the point of having them otherwise?'

Rosemary was quite religious, going to Mass weekly and she kept Lent. Josey was always making fun of her being so holy, but in fact Rosemary disagreed with the Church on contraception and abortion because 'it's a worse sin to bring an unwanted child into the world than have an abortion,' and she seemed to go to church more out of habit than anything else. When I had a sore throat Rosemary advised me to go to 'the Blessing of the Throat' at church on Wednesday nights, then grinned as she knew I wouldn't believe in it. She had a very strong sense of what was right and wrong, moral and immoral, what you should put up with and what you should complain about. Rosemary thought Josey and her friends were 'common' with all their swearing and drinking, and that drink was degrading in itself. She and Doreen often said that it was drunks in West London that gave the Irish a bad name, but their fathers and brothers weren't like that at all. Often our discussions were ethical, about what you should and shouldn't do, how to organise your life, what you could expect from a husband. She said that if a man mistreated you, then you should leave him; but boyfriends should pay for you when you go out, and Kevin always paid for her.

Rosemary stood up for herself, and never let anyone get away with using her or putting her down, whether it was the other women or the chargehand. She spoke out a lot during the dispute and everyone on the line wanted her to be our shop steward, because she was 'so bossy' and was bound to complain about everything and stand up for us. There were daily battles between her and Arlene; Arlene got very uppity if Rosemary sent a tray on before the right time and Rosemary complained bitterly about Arlene's cigarette smoke which billowed in our direction. It was constant telling off and in no uncertain terms, but they were great friends, too. Rosemary was friendly with Daphne as well, but wary of her moods and nosiness. She got on well with all the West Indian women, and was always asking Grace after Yvonne. She walked arm in arm with them, or put her arms round someone's neck if they were sitting down. I tensed up when she first did it to me but was soon doing the same myself.

Everyone respected Rosemary because she was so fair, always saw the good side in everyone, and was very kind and concerned. She had her work well organised and helped people out if they were 'up the wall' and she had a minute to spare, or she attached herself the clips or diodes that Grace and Alice had left out. From the firm's point of view, she was probably a good worker because she worked hard and picked up new jobs quickly, but again she had a very exact notion of what they were entitled to expect from her and what they weren't. She had Eamonn check the speed of the line practically every day, and would stop working altogether if her chair wasn't high enough or something was wrong with the jig. She thought the women who just 'made do' and didn't 'give out' were silly, as they would let the firm get away with anything and make conditions worse for the rest of us. She seemed to know instinctively what to put up with and what to resist, and during the dispute you could really rely on Rosemary's gut reactions to the situation and her interpretation of events.

There were eleven children in Rosemary's family; her father was a lorry driver. She was very attached to all her family and seemed to be writing letters to them at every spare minute, so she kept up with all their news. She was the third eldest, and her two older sisters were in America and Australia. Most of the Irish women at UMEC had brothers, or, more often, sisters who had emigrated in search of work, particularly to Australia. Rosemary was very excited when her 'American' sister came to London for a couple of days *en route* to Ireland for the first time in two years. The three eldest in Rosemary's family had had to leave home to get work. Her 17-year-old sister Geraldine and a 16-year-old friend came over from Ireland during the winter to look for hotel work in Jersey. When they couldn't find any Rosemary was very worried, sent them the fare to London and had the two of them living for several weeks in the small room with her and Doreen. Then she helped them find a flat and got them both jobs at UMEC. They worked two lines away from us. Rosemary kept going on about how young Geraldine was, and felt responsible for her to her mother. Letters flew backwards and forwards about whether Geraldine or Rosemary had a cold. Rosemary said her mother worried about all the children, and had to take tranquillisers when one left home, even though there were so many of them. She wouldn't have slept at all if she had known Geraldine hadn't found a job in Jersey. Not surprisingly, Rosemary and Doreen were both exhausted by having the other two stay with them.

There were nine girls and two boys, the eldest was twenty-six, and the baby, Sharon, was nine. Rosemary hated it over here when she first came, and cried for Sharon every night. She was very tied up with her sisters' problems, their new babies and houses though she hadn't seen them for over a year, and she bought Christmas and birthday presents for all of them. The two boys were both learning trades at technical college, but all the girls had left school at fifteen and gone straight into factory work, apart from the two who had clerical jobs abroad. For hours Rosemary would describe her life at home, and how everything was organised. Her mother cooked in the evening, and wouldn't make anything special if one of the children didn't like what she'd prepared. This led to a lengthy discussion up and down the line and with Doreen during the next break about whether you should cook different dinners for the different children's tastes, or make them eat what you've made. Her father cooked the breakfast and did all the weekend shopping, and the children took turns washing up. Whenever a new baby girl was born, her father would tell the others they'd got 'another washer upper'. When I saw photos of the whole family, I was surprised at how young her mother looked after having so many children. I told her that when I couldn't get to sleep at night I tried to think of the names of all her brothers and sisters.

Rosemary loved them all and didn't begrudge being poor because she wouldn't have the family any other way. She had never had a room to herself at home or here, but she seemed happier in a crowd than on her own. Some days she would put her head down on the line at lunchtime and go to sleep with us all talking around her, and she wasn't at all grumpy when she woke up but pleased to see us. She said how quiet and thoughtful her dad was, sitting in his chair or talking to the children, and she was especially fond of him because 'Mammy is very strong and could sort herself out in any situation but Daddy is so quiet.'

Most of the things Rosemary talked about were to do with her family and friends, and concrete problems of living; the only more general topic was sex. She was really quick and alert, but you could see how her horizons were limited by her hard life, and that she had next to no time to reflect on anything other than the most immediate problems and issues. She was terribly bored with the work and wouldn't stay there if she didn't have to, but she thought the only sort of job she would get in England was factory or shop work, because she was Irish and had no 'O' levels. If the opportunity arose, she would go after a clerical job, but she didn't want to risk losing her 'part-time' as she needed the money. Still, she was tied up all day and so busy that she wouldn't have had time even to look out for another job. She thought it was immoral for young girls to be working at UMEC. They were so exploited and got so tired that they couldn't enjoy being young. She was relieved when Geraldine left and went off to Jersey again. At twenty-three, Rosemary thought of herself as the older generation, and indeed she was very mature and responsible for her age – but then she had been working for nearly ten years.

Together on the line

All the women said 'good morning' to each other and acknowledged the others several times a day. The atmosphere was warm and supportive, so no one was left out. If you passed someone in the corridor or the loo whom you had seen a couple of times and just about recognised, you would say 'hello' to them. It was the same in the canteen: if you sat at a table with people you didn't know, you talked to them or at least said 'hello' and 'goodbye'. I never felt that I didn't belong, even though it was obvious I was different from the other women. Being white but not Irish was a great conversation starter. We chatted as much as the work allowed, but that didn't necessarily mean that everyone liked each other, as evidenced by Sharon and Joyce. Friendliness towards all the other women in the shop was automatic – because you were all in the same boat, doing the same work in the same place. It wasn't that they took a great personal liking to you as an individual on account of your personality, or because they identified with you. If someone was away or left, nobody mentioned her very much, and they wouldn't go out of their way to keep in contact with her. But while you were all there, you were best of friends.

Our discussions weren't competitive in the least. No one tried to score off each other, except Sharon with her showing off. Arlene and Rosemary were very firm with each other when they had one of their frequent differences of opinion, but they joked about it afterwards. Relationships between the women were so direct that they could sort out tensions as they arose, and clear the air straight away without building up hostile atmospheres. There was a constant issue of making sure the others didn't take liberties or treat you like a mug. At first I didn't want to answer people back. In professional jobs I had had before, there were other ways of distancing oneself from workmates, with sarcastic remarks and subtle hints, but I came to find it easy to express anger, and accuse them of all sorts of things, without feeling hostile. In my second week I had to stand up to Sharon: every morning when she brought the rolls she gave me a burnt one, or cheese instead of ham, quite apart from the fuss about my rejects. The others said she was renowned for all this, and I'd have to 'give out to her' to show her I wouldn't be bullied.

People judged each other more by how they behaved than by what they said, or what they thought. Joyce was always complaining about the union and how badly we were represented, but it was Rosemary whom the others wanted as shop steward, because they knew she would stand up for everyone on the line, even though she knew next to nothing about unions.

The solidarity gave you self-confidence. I was much more outgoing than I'd been for ages, and started conversations with people I'd never seen before, outside the factory as well as inside. I touched the others as much as they touched me without feeling at all awkward – it became quite natural to take someone's arm if you were walking in the same direction. You felt that everyone liked you being there, and this didn't depend on you saying something particularly stimulating or making an effort to be friendly. They looked after each other, and were quite concerned if someone felt ill. If you had a headache or period pains all the others knew, and Eileen would be told every month to go home instead of working in agony. When Rosemary got dermatitis she received lots of advice about what to say to the first aid, the doctor, and the union. They treated the others like part of the family so you couldn't imagine feeling left out. Everyone was included in what went on as a matter of course. I noticed how much I had changed when a new woman was brought to sit with me to learn modules. I took her up the line, introduced her to the others and showed her where everything was so she would feel at home. When I left, I made a point of seeking out people I didn't know very well but whom I'd met in the bikeshed, or at the hot water machine.

I felt quite rooted in the situation, although I found the lack of privacy a strain at first. Even when the work didn't force you to be in direct physical contact, like during the breaks, the women always wanted to sit together. Sometimes they were quiet or read the paper, but this was to distance themselves from the work and the line, not from each other. They liked to be with people the whole time, and weren't at all used to being on their own, so you were never intruding on their privacy.

Even though our line was so friendly the feeling of unity varied with how hard worked we were. After the dispute, when we were depressed and the work was extremely fast to make up for lost production, we were ratty with each other.

When we felt worn out or got 'up the wall' we took it out on the others, accusing them of not sending trays on regularly, or of forgetting pegs and clips. We all knew what was happening and that we shouldn't take it out on each other, but somehow we couldn't help it.

The same thing happened when we moved to a different line, and there was too little space and nowhere to put anything. We quarrelled about where the spare jigs should go when they weren't in use, and everyone tried to arrange things in the way most convenient for herself. The whole line seemed to disintegrate into a number of individuals, and nobody talked much for a few days. We all knew the pressure of the work was making us edgy and gradually we returned to normal.

On the 'old' line we had been united, quite unfairly, against the part-time evening workers whom we never saw. We acted as if they were a breed apart – dirty, lazy and thieving. Our cushions and vacuum flasks did disappear overnight, it was true, and in the morning we found our benches littered with cigarette ash, apple cores and sweet papers. Whatever 'build up' we had left was gone, and there were always several rejects to be seen to whereas we hadn't left any the night before. Everyone discouraged Ann and Nora from leaving any build up of calibrated basic mechanisms for the 'swing-shift', and I was advised to leave a few rejects for them to sort out. We gave out to Eamonn about the condition of the benches every time they had been working and told the supervisor to do something about them. Yet I'm sure that if we had known the women personally we would have been the best of friends.

When the line was at a low, the women divided more into ethnic groups than usual; the West Indians sat together, and so did the Irish. Being of the same national origin seemed to override personal likes and dislikes across the groups. Quite a few anti-black or Irish jokes would normally be made but always in fun, it seemed, and each joked about her own nationality or colour just as often.

The Indian women kept themselves to themselves more than the other ethnic groups; that was how it seemed, but maybe it was because the other women didn't talk much to them. The Indian women spoke Gujerati and Kutchi with each other. Most of them didn't speak English very well and were shy with the rest of us. Both the Irish and West Indian women had prejudices about them. They didn't positively dislike the Indian women – they didn't know them personally and were suspicious. On our line there were no Indian women, but during the dispute I got talking to Mrs Patel on the next line. She didn't seem used to talking to white women but then neither did I know many middle-aged Indian women. Once the ice was broken she was very friendly and we chatted every day. Her first name was Parvati but somehow it was easier to call her Mrs Patel as all the others did. The Indian women introduced themselves to the other ethnic groups as Mrs So-and-So and we addressed them as Mrs So-and-So – no doubt a sign of the distance between the Indian women and the others since everyone else automatically used first names. Mrs Patel said she hadn't worked when they first came to England, but now they couldn't manage on her husband's wage so she had to come out to work. He had just been on strike for five months so they were living on a shoestring. Her two children were at primary school and she got up at 5 every morning to do some housework before she came to work.

Prejudice against the Indian women was based on ignorance; they must be weak because they didn't eat meat, or they had to put olive oil on their hair and weren't allowed to wash it. Their religious taboos were condemned for being very restrictive. On our line, discussion of the Indian women revolved around arranged marriages, and how the women were beaten down by their husbands. It was generally believed that Indian men made their wives go out to work, forced them to do overtime, then took their pay packets at the end of the week. They thought the women were beaten up if their wages were lower than usual. All this probably came from their understanding of arranged marriages, because they thought the Indian women were kept completely under the thumb first of their family, then of their husband, and so never had any independence. They were pitied for their lack of freedom. One of the Indian women who had a secret lover was very popular with the Irish women because she had stuck up for herself. She spoke out against arranged marriages and was going to make sure her daughter didn't have to suffer one.

The more Anglicised the Indian women were, the less suspicion they aroused. Those who were very shy because they spoke little English were sometimes dismissed by the others as obedient sheep. A rumour went round during the dispute that one of the Indian women acted as leader and told the others which way to vote, and the rest did whatever she said. In fact the Indian women were the only group who sat it out right till the end, 'sitting in' all day every day; they never took the opportunity to skive off in the afternoon or go shopping. Some of them had relatives or friends who had been on strike at Grunwicks or Desoutters; they had a clear understanding of what was going on and of the need to stick it out as a group. They sat in a very colourful huddle, sewing sequins on the most beautiful coloured silk sarees for Diwali, 'our Christmas' as Mrs Patel called it. One of them was knitting a striped red and white scarf for her daughter who was a Liverpool supporter. One day I was sent by Arlene and Rosemary to ask about the coloured dots on their forehead. Mrs Patel explained they were to match the colour of their sarees, so settling a lot of speculation about why it wasn't always a red dot. They must have found us very ignorant, and they giggled at our silly questions.

Irish women who worked on the same line as Indian women became quite friendly when they knew them personally, and then these preconceptions disappeared. One elderly Irish woman from the specialist shop off the main assembly worked next to me for a few days. She was in a terrible muddle about her tax and holiday money, and while I helped her sort them out, she started talking about the young Indian woman she normally sat next to. I was surprised at her explanation of Indian extended families. She thought it was very convenient for working mothers because aunties and grannies looked after the children so they didn't need to worry about them while they were out at work. All the shopping and cooking was done for them, so it was much easier really than living on their own with their husbands and having to do all the housework. She seemed quite persuaded that arranged marriages were preferable to ours.

Suspicions about marriage and men were like the first line of racial prejudice. Each group prided itself on standing up to its own men better than the others. The West Indians made comments about the Irish women, similar to those the Irish women made about the Indians. Their husbands were boors, bossed the women round, sent them out to work, took their money and drank it away. The West Indians thought the Irish women were weak for not standing up to their men. When Rosemary got engaged, Arlene whispered to me that 'he's engaging her to her doom', and she was very suspicious of the way Irish couples organised their homes. Grace, Daphne and Arlene laughed at the engagements and big white weddings the Irish went in for – they were 'so old-fashioned'.

Among the West Indian women at UMEC were several single mothers. They said they'd become strong through standing up for themselves and they thought the Irish women didn't like children, but 'left the breeding to us black women'. I said it just looked like that in the factory because the Irish women gave up work when they had babies while Arlene and Grace had carried on working when their children were small; but Arlene wouldn't have it.

Arlene lumped 'natives' and West Indians in one group as English, and thought that conditions would be much better in UMEC if there were more of 'us', as 'we' wouldn't tolerate the conditions that some of the Irish women put up with. The West Indian women generally held the Irish responsible for the poor working conditions. 'Us English' were prepared to stand up for ourselves but they would stay all night if the supervisor told them to, or sit on the floor to do the work. Needless to say, this went along with saying the Irish were stupid – 'they must be to accept these conditions'. Stories were told of Irish women who had shown off to the supervisors by trying to do more work than was necessary; Ann was despised for making such a large build-up because it wouldn't get her anywhere, and Sharon was thought a sneak for sucking up to the chargehands. All this was cited as evidence that the Irish women didn't know where their interests lay.

There was an element of truth in this. Many of the new young women were straight over from Ireland and often in their first factory job. They did as they were told without complaining, and this could make the job worse for the next person. It only showed how vulnerable the young Irish women were and that the West Indian women were much more accustomed to industrial life. They'd also come from rural areas but by now they'd all been working in factories for over a decade. Irish women who had been there for some years and knew the score, agreed with the West Indians. Doreen, Rosemary's flatmate, thought that management could get away with almost anything because 'all these new girls off the banana boat from Cork' would do whatever they were told, and never challenge anything.

The Irish blamed 'the others' generally for the bad conditions, regardless of ethnic origin. 'You know the girls here, they just won't stand up for themselves,' said Rosemary. 'They'll all complain but they won't do anything about it.' This wasn't strictly true either and, when it came to it, the Irish women were just as vociferous as the West Indians.

Sometimes they put down their own nationality. Doreen went on about 'drunken Paddies' staggering from pub to pub and giving the Irish a bad name. She assured the rest of us that the men weren't like that at home. When the West Indians said 'we're only black but. . . .' it was always tongue in cheek, or ironic, like the time Arlene criticised Kathleen for complaining to the chargehand that the line was going too slow: 'I know I'm just a monkey up a tree, but these Irish are really stupid.' Any discussion about the slave-trade and British colonialism was turned round to 'prove' that the British got the worst deal. 'They called it slavery but the whites did all the work. Look at it now – at home you can have an easy life sitting in the sun, smoking ganja, picking fruit off the trees, and it's only the whites who are beavering away at work.' Arlene said she didn't know what work was till she came here, and 'look how all the natives are killing themselves with heart attacks from overwork'. There was a lot of joking about blacks being straight out of the jungle and the Irish being thick. Each group often accused the other of not speaking English properly and imitated their accents.

The Irish women thought that I was Irish, but the West Indians thought I was different because I wasn't as pale as the Irish. Each told me what they thought about the other group, and when they were in conflict I had to decide which side I'd line up with. If the line was at a real low there was no question about it – I was definitely treated as one of the Irish. On one occasion, Arlene and Alice had a long wrangle with Rosemary about St Patrick. They said he was black and she said he was white. Her mother had a picture of him, Rosemary said, and he was 'a dear old man, with a stick and a beard' and he was white. Anyway 'they wouldn't have a black man as patron saint of Ireland'. When they asked me, I made it worse by saying that many people thought Jesus was a black man. That started them off again because Arlene said of course Jesus was black, and Rosemary thought she was being ridiculous.

The Irish women didn't seem to be prejudiced against the West Indians except when it came to their food. I was surprised because they couldn't have had much contact with black people at home. There were close friendships across the ethnic groupings, and they took care to avoid using racist words. One Irish woman apologised to Alice during the dispute for referring to someone as a 'blackleg' but Alice wasn't offended. Sometimes one of them would exclaim that we were being worked 'like blacks', and then took great pains to explain that they meant it was like slave-labour and what had happened to black people in the past, and that they didn't mean anything rude by it. The Irish thought it was good that the black women didn't stick together as much as the Indians, and that they judged people 'for what they are, not whether they are black or white'. The others often asked after Grace's daughter and everyone was interested in Alice's grandchildren. Eileen and Rosemary were curious about how the West Indians lived and 'what it's like where you come from'. The West Indians thought them ignorant – they didn't even know about the different islands in the Caribbean and couldn't distinguish between different accents. Arlene often said she was glad to talk to me because I was more 'international minded'.

Doreen said I was silly to be working in a factory with all my schooling. If her parents had been able to afford it, she would also have had a better training but there were too many children. Anyway, there were so few jobs at home, she said, that Irish girls had to come over here and get whatever work they could find. Education was a common topic of conversation on the line. Once the West Indian women spent the whole day discussing why schools were better at home than here, and how come children went to school for a shorter time than here but came out more educated. All possible explanations were thoroughly discussed, and they asked me what it was like being a teacher, whether the kids were more difficult to teach at certain ages, and whether boys were really naughtier than girls. They all made their own children stay on at school after the minimum school leaving age, and were strict about homework. Pearl, another West Indian woman on the next line told me proudly that her neighbour's daughter was training to be a doctor, and her own daughter was doing 'O' levels. Pearl barred her from doing housework, and made her stay in till 9 p.m. every night to do homework. None of the black women wanted their daughters to do factory work, and were very keen for them to get qualifications. Doreen and Rosemary agreed that parents should make sure their daughters received a good education, especially if there were only a few children in the family.

Everyone thought the jobs on the line were an insult to our intelligence and despised the way the men spoke down to us, 'as if we were as stupid as their jobs'. The West Indian and Irish women agreed that if you were born over here, you could get a better job than UMEC, but being immigrants they didn't possess the necessary paper qualifications for better jobs and had had to take manual work. They wouldn't have stayed if they had an alternative.

Anna

Anna was often called 'the German woman'. She was of German origin, in her early fifties, and started at UMEC a couple of months before me. The rest of her family also worked there; her husband Frank drove a forklift trolley in the goods inwards where he was a chargehand, and her 17-year-old daughter Jill had been in the main assembly for a year-and-a-half, ever since she left school. By training Anna was a dressmaker, but hadn't worked outside the home since Jill was born. They were both on different lines from me, but we became close because of our common interest in working out the number of UMOs produced and UMEC's profits, and because they, like me, did not belong to any of the main national groupings.

After the dispute Anna became very concerned about 'what the firm is getting away with', and came over to me every day to find out from the *Guardian* how UMEC's shares had done the day before. If they had gone down she said it was because we had slowed down the day before or there had been a hold up, and when they had gone up it was because the supervisor had really pushed us with the bonus rate. She invented all kinds of motives on the part of the supervisor and managers for squeezing us even more. Rosemary and Arlene would groan when Anna approached at lunchtime 'because she's going to yap about profits again'. Sometimes she bought her own 'big' paper, as all those apart from the *Sun* and *Mirror* were known, even the 'pink' one.

Anna watched all the changes in the place so that we would know what the firm was up to, and we discussed the speed ups and harder pace of work. Once when the top managers brought visitors from a European motor company to inspect the new line which she was working on, she called over the works manager and in front of all the men asked him not to forget the back pay they owed us. This was very brave, but most of the women thought she was nuts, and the shop steward warned her she would soon be 'in the office' if she carried on like that. In fact, the supervisor and the managers came over to her after the visitors had left to ask what message she had for the works manager. Much to our amazement, she repeated it. Anna was an unlikely looking militant, very respectable with an apron over her tweed skirt, and pink National Health spectacles.

Some of the others thought she and her family must be 'money mad', all working in the factory, and they pitied Jill for having been there since she left school. 'Surely they could afford to have kept her on at school as she was the only child.' Jill hated work, and on bad days went home in tears, completely worn out, but she wouldn't respond to any suggestions about alternative jobs, or day release. She thought she would stay at UMEC till she got married, at about twenty-four. It was strange to hear her say that as she hadn't yet had a boyfriend. Jill was still a child in some ways, but also world-weary and mature in her attitude to work. She too was militant in the dispute. Anna felt she was protecting Jill at work, preventing the chargehands from exploiting the young girls even more than they did, and she made sure Jill never learned calibrating, because she was convinced that the magnetic box ruined your health.

The family was certainly not 'money mad'. Frank had a nervous breakdown the previous year due to constant worry about paying the rent and bills, as he just couldn't earn enough for them to live on. After he had been in hospital, he finally agreed that Anna should come out to work as well. Life was much easier now that the three of them were working, and they could make ends meet.

Frank was Jewish, and came from Germany as a youth in the 1930s. For many years, he worked as a pastrycook. Then he went to a large food factory for a bit; Anna couldn't stand him smelling of vinegar all the time and got fed up with having to wash his underwear so often because of the smell, so he left and came to UMEC. Frank was in his mid-fifties, a nervy person, but very warm and friendly. His main interest in life was his allotment, and he often brought me leeks and Brussels sprouts. He wasn't interested in the union, and the two women said they couldn't discuss the dispute at home, only on the bus on the way to work. He came over to my bench to say hello whenever he visited his wife and daughter on the shopfloor.

Anna had spent the war on a farm in Germany. Her father had died young, and her mother, who was Catholic, married a Jewish man. In the 1930s, the stepfather was sent to a concentration camp by the Nazis, but managed to escape while he was being taken from the camp to hospital with an infected foot. The mother, stepfather and younger brother came to England in 1939 on a visitor's visa, the stepfather on a false passport. They stayed here and sent for Anna but war broke out and it was too late for her to come. She was sent with other 'orphans' to live and work on a farm. She was there between the ages of ten and fifteen so her schooling was completely disrupted, and she told horrific stories of how the farmer tried to rape the young girls, and how she had tricked him in front of his wife. After the war, she left everything and came to England to join her family. She had worked as a dressmaker in small sweatshops but she thought the wages in the rag trade were so low now that she might as well be with Jill at UMEC.

All three were extremely kind to me. As well as the vegetables, Anna kept bringing me huge chunks of homemade cheesecake, and the most delicious marzipan cake. She gave me so much that anything I gave her in return like flapjack seemed measly by comparison. Before Christmas, I had flu and was off for two weeks, and I didn't get paid when I came back, as there was no sick pay. On the Thursday, payday, I was talking to Anna when she stuffed a £10 note into my trouser pocket so quickly I wasn't even really sure what it was. She was giving it to me because I would be short, having lost two weeks' wages, and she refused point blank to take it back. She had had a tax rebate and had even managed to put aside a few pounds in the building society, so she insisted it wouldn't make any difference to her, and it was a gift not a loan. I tried to return it, but it almost turned into me insulting her by not accepting her generosity; in the end I let it go for a few days, asking the others how on earth I could give it back. Eventually, I dropped the £10 note into her apron pocket the next Thursday, and ran off before she could give it back again. I was quite overwhelmed by her generosity; the gift was completely genuine and she really didn't want the money back. The whole attitude to money and seeing that others had got enough was so different from my previous job where although we earned much more, people remembered who owed whom a cup of coffee. All the women were very generous, sharing out sweets and crisps and whatever they bought for themselves, but Anna's generosity went further than most.

Frank was worried about me getting tired out from the work, and wanted to inquire about clerical jobs for me. Now that they had a bit more money they were saving for a house.

Frank had lived in the same flat for thirty years. It had no toilet or bathroom, and they had to bath in a zinc tub, filled with water boiled in the kettle. He didn't mind the conditions, but objected to the fact that he had paid for the house many times over in rent over the years, yet he had no security at all, especially for when he retired. Even if he had enough money to buy the house he wouldn't be able to afford to renovate it. Their dream was to buy a small house with a garden; he said, that they had all discussed it and agreed that when they got it they wanted me to come and be their lodger. I was very touched, and felt quite guilty about my flat which was like a mansion compared to theirs.

Josey

Josey came from a large unruly Irish family, with six children all spaced a year apart. She had her eighteenth birthday while at UMEC, and her eldest sister who had emigrated to Australia was only twenty-two. They had come over from Tipperary when Josey was six, and lived locally ever since. She put on an Irish accent at will, and thought of herself as Irish, but she was really quite different from the girls straight over from Ireland.

Josey wouldn't accept authority. She larked around all the time, and made fun of the older women who took the work seriously. She was noisy, and laughed so loud everyone got annoyed, and made raucous chicken-clucking noises most afternoons. If she started before lunchtime, she said she was 'laying early today'. Sometimes she went drinking at midday, and would come tottering back, usually after clocking-in time, even noisier than usual. She hated the job, and did her best to keep herself and the rest of us amused with her refusal to buckle under. Some days she made 'bean bag people', filling the cotton work gloves with metal washers, tying up the wrists with a rubber band, and drawing funny faces on them. She sent them up the line in a tray and then cackled at our surprise to find a bean bag person on top of the UMO. She hollered to her friend two lines away to discuss the 'fellas' they'd gone out with the night before.

Josey annoyed the other women as well by working so slowly that she got everyone else 'up the wall', or by switching the fan on and off. One day she was so 'up the wall' herself that there were trays on the floor – unheard of – as well as piled up on the benches in front and behind her. The line had to be stopped for half an hour and two more girls brought over to sort it out; one of them turned out to be a friend of hers, and they got into a mock fight pushing each other over on top of the UMOs, until Eamonn lost his temper and the rest of the shop was tut-tutting at her. If she didn't like a particular task she just wouldn't do it, which eventually cost her her job. In any case, she was always on the lookout for other work, and I helped her answer an advert for traffic wardens which she thought would be good as she could blackmail offenders for the fine, and tell off men. She had worked in shops and at a dry cleaners before, and after UMEC she got a full-time job as an office junior, as well as a part-time one calling out the numbers in a bingo hall.

Josey's home life struck us as riotous. Her parents were separated and each lived with someone else. All the children lived with the mother, her new man and numerous dogs. Her mother worked full-time but cooked a different meal for each child as it arrived home from school or work, and did all the housework. She encouraged Josey to go drinking and would join her on Saturday mornings, telling the others that they were going out to do the shopping. They often got blind drunk, Josey downing Pernod and lemonade at a rate of knots, and completely forgot the shopping. Many mornings she came to work with a hangover or bruised knees from having been dragged home, or having lost one of her shoes.

Josey had had many boyfriends and was currently going out with a divorced man twice her age with four children of his own. His wife was in Ireland but his youngest 5-year-old daughter was over here with him; somehow she had been palmed off on Josey's mum. This man beat up Josey occasionally, and the rest of the line thought her stupid for having anything to do with him. Everyday there were jokes about bruises and love bites, especially if she was wearing a polo neck sweater. She was more sexually experienced than the girls straight over from Ireland; they thought she was 'terrible common', and pretended to be shocked whenever she swore, which was most of the time. She in turn thought them narrow minded, and old-fashioned, and used to tease Rosemary for being so 'holy' when Rosemary tutted at the swearing and chicken-clucking. She was always running out of money and had to borrow from her mum. But she was very generous, handing out sweets and chocolate whenever she bought them. She didn't offer them, but handed them to you and you couldn't refuse or she got quite angry.

Josey hated school, and said she left when she was only fourteen, telling the teachers that she was going back to Ireland, but in fact she had worked since then. She was certainly tougher and more worldly that the other school leavers. However, one of her favourite occupations was writing poetry, and some of her poems were quite good. She'd written them in an exercise book and read them out to everyone. Mostly they were romantic or funny, but some of them shocked the others who thought they were too 'dirty'. She asked me to show her how to join the public library and take books out of the poetry section. She also loved to have 'a good discussion' – mostly about men, marriage (she was never going to get married but wanted eleven children), and what was in the paper. She became very serious about the things that really interested her. Although she was keen on men, she preferred going out to drink with her 'mates' because 'you could have a good talk with them'.

Everyone was fond of Josey though at times we all were irritated by her. I could have killed her one day when she kept turning off the fan just to annoy me but I couldn't do anything about it as the switch was on her side of the line.

Life outside

We chatted about everything under the sun while we were working. The older women talked a lot about the past and what it was like at home in Ireland or the West Indies. There were often political or philosophical debates: we poured over the newspapers every day and discussed what was going on in the world, in Zimbabwe and the Common Market, what we thought of Mrs Thatcher, and various industrial disputes. The topics were constrained by the news coverage in the *Sun* and *Mirror*, and the scandal about Princess Margaret and Roddy Llewellyn kept us going for several days; everyone took her side against the Queen and thought she should be left to lead her own life in peace. Last night's telly was dissected, and then we got onto the nitty-gritty of how to lead our lives. The same questions came up time and time again – what was the best age to get married and how many children should you have? How much should you let men get away with? Was it right to have an abortion if you were married? The younger women, all of whom were Irish, intended to have smaller families than their mothers, and thought there was no point getting married unless you wanted children. So it wouldn't be fair on your husband to have an abortion – it was quite a different matter though if you didn't want children in the first place. Many stories were told of what had happened at the doctor's and at the family planning clinic.

One day Doreen asked me 'what's the difference between vasectomy and hysterectomy?' after she'd been reading an agony column, and a bit later 'what's anal intercourse?' They weren't familiar with the words but all knew what it was when I explained. Then Rosemary asked how the Pill worked, and whether you could use the coil before you've had a baby. They treated me as a general source of information on these matters, but I think it was also a way of testing me out. I was the odd one out, being older and unmarried but more openminded than the older women, and they wanted to find out what I was really like. Their questions always had a moral or ethical twist, no doubt influenced by their Catholic backgrounds. I was quite cautious in my replies until I got to know them well. I thought they would oppose abortion on principle, and didn't want to offend them, but in fact they all agreed with Rosemary that the church was way behind the times on everything to do with sex.

Family and home were the most important things in their lives. As they saw it, your life consists of two parts, home and work, and you want to have a happy home life to make up for the work. They were curious about how other people lived, and wanted detailed accounts of friends of mine who lived communally, had more than one sexual relationship, or were living together but not married. They weren't nosy or disapproving, but really wanted to know how it worked. I had to explain exactly how I sorted out the finances with the people in my flat.

For them, living differently wasn't a practical possibility; they knew only what they were used to and had little knowledge of how other people lived apart from what they'd seen on television. Their own experiences were dictated by pressure of work, lack of time and physical exhaustion. They had a hard time just keeping up with the basic household chores, and the straight and narrow. Experimenting with more 'open' relationships, trying to live communally or not as a couple, require time, energy and discussion that weren't at their disposal. They were quite openminded about communes and homosexuality but other people's more exotic lives were beyond their horizons. The little spare time they had was spent in much-needed relaxation, and the only real breaks of the year were Christmas and the two weeks' summer holiday. You just couldn't imagine trying to alter your basic approach to family life when you were tied down like that.

The women with children had even fewer options, and most of them had a child by the time they were twenty-four. The Irish women tended to stay at home when their children were small, but Sharon and a couple of others didn't; they took their children to baby minders at 7 a.m. and collected them again in the evening. At 7 a.m. the High Street was full of mums, taking young children to baby minders.

Doing the job just for money made the young girls look forward to marriage and children as a release from the work. Discussions about training for a better job or demanding day release were just so much idle talk, because most of them wouldn't do anything about it. Realistically getting married and having a baby would be the major change in their life. They were always going to engagement parties and weddings, and saved up for months to buy a new outfit; they were really excited if one of their sisters or cousins had a baby. They looked blankly at me when I said that I'd never got married because I wanted 'my independence'. It just didn't make sense to them. When they knew me better, I went into it in more detail, and they saw how many options and choices a professional job could give you, just through the extra time and money. Their attitude to children was different as well. They expected to have children as a matter of course, whereas for women in the circles I had moved in it was always an agonising choice between children, on the one hand, and a job and 'independence', on the other. In the factory there was no independence or career to conflict with having children, and they couldn't imagine them being an intrusion in your life. It was simply a question of when, rather than whether, to have them.

This meant it wasn't such a disaster to get pregnant before you really wanted. If you didn't want a child, or didn't want to settle down yet, that was your business, and you should 'get rid of it'. But at the back of their minds they thought women who didn't have any children were selfish, and they couldn't understand liking children but not wanting your own. When we realised that Maureen was pregnant, I thought it was terrible for her to be tied down so young but the others reacted differently. Rosemary thought Maureen was stupid to have kept it, because 'her boyfriend might leave her and anyway he's a bowsie [drinker]'. But for Maureen herself it was only a matter of time – it didn't matter that much whether she had a baby now or in three years' time.

There was a tremendous amount of discussion about all these issues, and most of the younger women had planned out their lives. They knew how many children they wanted and when. They were familiar with the pros and cons of different methods of contraception. Most of them intended to stay at home until the youngest child reached school age, and then go back to work. It struck me forcefully that material circumstances quite beyond their control made family and children the most important things in their lives.

In a way, the emphasis on marriage was misleading. They seemed much more concerned about having a family and a home of their own than about marrying a particular man.

The division between the sexes appeared to be as strong outside the factory as inside. Their closest relationships were with other women, rather than with their boyfriends, and most of their social gatherings seemed to be all female. Josey wasn't alone in going out with a gang of girls. Doreen and Rosemary went dancing together, and so did Eileen and Ann. Before they quarrelled, the two deaf and dumb women had been inseparable. Even after they were married, the women went out for an evening together without their husbands and seemed much more at ease in the company of women than men. And, of course, the men also had their own single-sex social life in the pub.

In some ways, Maureen was closer to Josey than to her 'fella', and Rosemary seemed as close to Doreen as to Kevin. Indeed, they spent so much time with each other that they sounded like a married couple when they discussed what chores needed doing at home. Domestic life and money matters must have been sorted out between a married couple, but outside the home social life seemed to be almost exclusively single sex. The younger ones seemed much more tied up with each other emotionally than middle-class girls of the same age. From what I remembered of being a student, in the days before the women's movement, as soon as you acquired a boyfriend he became the most important relationship, and girlfriends were dropped; you only went out with other women as a second best.

For the young Irish women in the factory, this division between the sexes carried over into all spheres of life. They had very definite views about what sort of work was fitting for a man; building work and hard physical labour was much more 'manly' than working in a factory. Rosemary's two brothers were both apprentices, and she and Doreen thought that boys ought to learn a trade; whether girls were trained or not would depend on whether the parents could go on supporting them, but the boys took priority. After all, they said, the boys would have to support a family eventually and they'd need to earn a decent wage.

I had a set-to with Doreen one morning about wiring plugs. Her hair dryer had broken and she thought the plug had gone, and wanted a man to fix on a new one. I said she should learn how to do it herself; it was much easier than a lot of the jobs we did on the line. But she said no, she wasn't going to learn, because there'd always be a 'fella' around who could do it. If there wasn't, she'd lean out the window and call to the nearest man in the street to help her. I was taken aback, but then she couldn't see why I made an issue of it. She had all sorts of other ideas about jobs that men should do and jobs that women should do; she thought each sex should only do what they specialised in, and should not intrude on the other sex's sphere. This didn't include shopping, cooking or washing, but women did sewing and mending, and men did woodwork and electrics. She wasn't going to learn about wiring, as she had quite enough to do already; men weren't likely to learn how to sew, so she would end up doing everything if she learnt all the men's jobs as well as the women's. Our argument must have convinced her that I was a bit odd, and the next day she came and asked why I wore flat shoes and added 'don't you ever wear high heels?'

Doreen wasn't alone in these views. All the young women agreed with her, also they all thought that if you went out with a 'fella', he should pay for you, like Kevin did for Rosemary. She didn't need to spend a penny all weekend - he paid for all the meals, cinema, fares, and he gave her presents as well. Doreen thought Kevin would make Rosemary a good husband. They didn't think that women were inferior to men, or men were more clever. Nor did they think that if a 'fella' paid for you he was entitled to any rights over you or your body. Their views sprang from the reality of women's lives. Their experience had always been different from men, at school, at work and at home. In a way, Doreen was protecting her own sphere – life was hard enough without wiring plugs and putting up shelves as well.

Chapter Five
The division of labour

If you were a woman you could walk into the factory on your sixteenth birthday, get a job on the assembly line, and stay there till you retired at sixty. There was no promotion off the line, so the highest position you could hope for would be 'reject operating', filling in when another woman was away, and mending the rejects.

Almost all the women on the shopfloor were 'operators', and all the operators were women, so women were overwhelmingly in the same grade. They were practically all immigrants as well, young women just over from Ireland like Geraldine, Rosemary's sister, or older women who had come to England from India and the West Indies, like Alice and Grace. If you'd just left school in London and had some CSEs, they might have offered you an office job with higher pay and shorter hours like the personnel manager offered me. If you'd been to school in the West Indies, India or had just come over from Ireland, you had no chance of clerical work.

Practically all the clerical workers in the wages and personnel offices were English, including some young black women. It didn't seem to matter what colour the clerical workers were so long as they'd gone to school here and reached whatever standard of spoken and written 'Queen's English' the personnel office required.

In a high immigrant area like West London, UMEC had a constant supply of cheap female labour and could take its pick of workers. Most of the women who looked there for work had a sister or friend already working at UMEC and knew from the grapevine that work was available. All the local factories as far as the large Victoria Trading Estate used this same pool of workers and the women always knew whether there were vacancies at other factories and how their pay and conditions compared with ours. Veronica, a 19 year old from Galway, with bright red hair who looked about fourteen had just left a confectionery factory after two years when she joined our line. She thought the pay would be better at UMEC. In fact she found our work ten times harder; they hadn't had to clock on where she worked before, had longer breaks and got weekly vouchers for cheap packets of sweets which she missed. Several of Rosemary's friends left to work at a foreign-owned engineering firm on the Victoria Trading Estate also doing assembly work but with no line or light; the women worked in small groups 'in their own time' and the pay was £10 a week more than ours even after deductions.

The West Indian women on my line had all been at UMEC for a long time, between ten and thirteen years, and would stay till they retired. Their years of service entitled them to 'staff status' – sick pay and a few more days' holiday than the rest of us. Staff status for operators used to start after ten years but this had recently been reduced to two years. Office workers and most of the men got it straight away. The West Indian women had done unskilled or semi-skilled work ever since they had been in England, and all were making sure their daughters would be qualified for office work.

The Indian women had settled in Britain more recently than the West Indian women and were younger, in their thirties and forties. Working at UMEC was the first employment outside the home for most of them since they had been here, as it was for Mrs Patel. In general, women from the Indian subcontinent seemed to get an even worse deal in local jobs than Irish or black women – they were concentrated in small or ununionised factories or those with very low pay. Because of their lack of industrial work experience and lack of English, employers were able to treat them either as the least desirable or as the most exploitable source of labour.

When I started in the factory there were no English school leavers working on the lines at all – neither black nor white. Most of the younger women came from Ireland. The majority of them had left home and come to England between the ages of sixteen and twenty-five. Once they'd started on the line, they had little chance of getting a better job at UMEC or anywhere else. I can't imagine that their level of education was lower than local school leavers, but they hadn't been able to get a job at home because of unemployment so left to look for work here, only to go to the bottom of the pile for their age group. Geraldine and Veronica were much more 'respectable' than Josey and got on better with their work, but they hadn't dreamt of trying for office work, while she got her job as an office junior quite easily. The young Irish women wanted to stay in England for only a few years. Some did go home, but in fact most of them stayed longer than they had originally intended; many married Irish building workers and settled down in West London. Like the West Indians and Indians they had come because of unemployment and there hadn't been much improvement in the situation at home to go back to.

By the time I had been in the factory for six months, there were about fifteen school leavers, all white. As jobs became harder to find they came to UMEC: it was either that or going straight on the dole – presumably that was where more of the black and Asian school leavers ended up. At UMEC you got the feeling that the younger women were trapped until they got married or had a baby. The firm didn't tell them about day release or offer them any sort of training.

The Sex Discrimination Act seemed to have made no inroad into the job structure whatsoever. Arlene said there used to be boys on the line and even a few women supervisors; but the week before the Equal Pay Act became law, everyone was shunted round so all the assembly line workers would be women, and all the supervisors and higher grades would be men, and they wouldn't have to pay higher rates to women. Even in the machine shop where both men and women worked, the women were paid at a lower rate on the grounds that they couldn't lift heavy coils of metal and had to use the services of labourers with trolleys.

The division was most glaring between the young girls and men. If you were a 16-year-old boy you would automatically be trained even if only to be a chargehand. The girls weren't even given the choice. But they weren't in a position to challenge this; if they didn't like the job they were offered the firm could say they didn't have to take it and could go somewhere else.

The women were all in the same grade as semi-skilled assemblers, except for Margaret the training woman, one woman chargehand, and a few women at the lowest level of quality control. The position of the men was totally different: there were white English men as well as immigrants, though virtually no white English women; the men were spread through many different grades, from labourer to manager, and were divided from each other by differences of skill and pay, as well as from us. They didn't form a single group like the women. All the men had some training and a career structure of sorts, apart from the labourers. They were paid more than us, had better working conditions and received staff status from the beginning. They filled all the grades and different categories of work other than assembler. So they were not a homogeneous group – but from where we were on the line, anyone with skill or training was a man, anyone in authority was a man, and any man had authority. We were wary of them all, even the maintenance electricians, because they were so much higher and could report us to the supervisor if they saw us eating or reading outside the break-times.

I knew the sexual division would be like that, but it still shook me every day. You could see the differences so clearly on the shopfloor: everyone who was working was a woman, and the men in their white coats were standing around chatting, humping skips or walking about to check the number of components. It was obvious that the only qualification you needed for a better job was to be a man. Many of the women wore bright overalls, pink, blue or green, but the men were in white except the labourers who wore brown coats. If any woman on the line was getting too bossy they'd say she was 'after a white coat', a comment frequently made about Sharon, our reject operator. Anyone in a suit was higher than a white coat – an engineer or a manager – and they ignored us completely.

It took me some time to sort out the different groups of men and how they fitted into the hierarchy. The women knew only the jobs of men with whom they came into direct contact, and weren't in a position to differentiate between the others. In any case, they weren't particularly interested, as all the men were the same from their point of view – higher up.

We were friendliest with the labourers, whose job was moving our empty skips and boxes, and collecting the rubbish. They were either old and ill, or mentally subnormal. Alf was Scottish and had a heart condition, and another man with a bad heart died while I was there. I didn't know how to behave towards Kenny and Ron, the two backward labourers, when I first started, but the women and the charge-hands were all very affectionate towards them. Kenny was about twenty-two although he seemed much younger, and looked quite normal apart from the way he walked. He liked to come and have a chat, but once he'd sat down would never go away. Ron was older, a small roly-poly man with black hair who played the clown. People were always cuddling him and giving him sweets, and even the supervisor often put his arm round him. The women sent Ron on errands to the 'back shop' just outside the factory gate, to buy them a banana or packet of crisps, and keep the change. They weren't supposed to but the chargehands turned a blind eye. We didn't trust Alf nearly so much because he was very moody and could be a 'sneak'.

We were also more or less on a par with the 'workmen' – maintenance men, mechanics and electricians – who dealt with broken-down machines. Even though they were quite friendly, you still couldn't be sure of them. Most were English; there were a few Asians, but no black maintenance men. I imagined their jobs were similar to some of the women's husbands' jobs. They treated us as if we could have been their wives or daughters; you could have a joke with them. After I got to know the Asian electrician who came to mend my checking machine on a number of occasions, I would tell him 'to take his time' mending it, so I could have a bit of a rest. The workmen's jobs seemed much easier than ours because they weren't tied to the line and didn't have to work at speed.

It was easy to see the hierarchy of the production workers:

on the bottom us 'girls', then a chargehand for each line, above him a section supervisor, and then the supervisor. There was a German and a Spanish chargehand but the rest were Irish men who had settled here. Their job was to administer the line, see it ran smoothly, order components before they ran out, lug skips to the women and supervise changeovers from one set to another. They were the first line of authority, switching on the line again as soon as the tea-break was over, and sending you to the supervisor if you did something against the rules. To us they seemed very powerful, but apparently they couldn't even get us more workgloves without having their order countersigned by the supervisor, and they didn't make any decisions at all. They just had to follow the layout for each set, which detailed the jobs. When a different UMO was to be assembled all they had to do was to come and rearrange us and tell us what to do. The progress chasers decided in advance how many UMOs were to be made up in each batch, and if the components ran out it was their responsibility, not the chargehands'. But the chargehands were in control of setting the light and the line speed.

Eamonn, our chargehand, was easy-going and a bit lazy. He didn't hassle us much, but then most of the women had been doing the job for years and years and knew what should be done much better than he. The more efficient chargehands bossed the women on their line much more and were very distant, especially if they were after promotion and wanted the supervisor to notice them.

Kurt, the German chargehand on the next line, was bossy and shouted a lot – he made life hell for 'his girls', especially Mrs Patel. He used to shriek at her if she sent a reject along the line or left oil smudges on the inside of the aluminium cover. He was quite openly racist about the Indian women and muttered about them all the time. When he wasn't rushing around shouting so the supervisor could hear how efficient he was, Kurt sat hawk-eyed at the top of the line. We all thought his behaviour pathetic, and naturally the women on his line were pretty uncooperative with him. Anna said he was like the SS. He was only about thirty, but was large, with a loud voice, so quite imposing. Once when I was put on his line to check the tightness of screws on the new Continental sets, I told him which airgun further down the line was the one that wasn't tightening them hard enough. He called over the engineer and the supervisor to tell them what *he'd* noticed. We were pleased when he had to go into hospital with back trouble.

Edna, the woman chargehand, was much nicer, but couldn't bear her line to be stopped even for a second. She was known for pushing 'her girls' more than the men did. It would have been a very heavy job if you were small or not used to lifting heavy weights, but Edna was big and strong. The women thought her unfeminine; no one said they thought she was a lesbian (they were quite open about saying someone looked 'bent'), but they were definitely surprised when Edna got married. Her line was right in the centre of the shopfloor and did sets for foreign vehicles. Anna's daughter, Jill, worked on it and that's why she got so tired out. Carol, the shop steward for all the women, did the build up of the basic mechanism on it and we could all see her at the front of the line. As the months wore on Edna seemed to acquire all the new school leavers who started work.

Both Kurt and Edna knew how many components each operator had and when they were likely to run out, and anticipated this by ordering a new lot from the stores. They also lifted the boxes into position in front of the women, and went round helping to unload components from large skips into small boxes so the women wouldn't have to jump up and down the whole time and interrupt their work.

But on our line, when we ran out of something we'd have to shout to Eamonn three or four times before he brought something more, and it meant yelling really loud because he was usually sitting at the top of the line rather than wandering round. If you ran out of modules or transistors, your trays would pile up in front of you while he went to fetch more; he wouldn't stop the line to help you get 'down the wall', so you'd have to work extra hard just because he was lazy. He didn't lift up the boxes either, but left them lying on the ground, so you had to jump up every few minutes to change an empty box for a full one or refill a small box. This was very inconvenient, as I discovered when I was putting the diactor and three covers on the Princess, because there were so many boxes running out all the time. If you wanted him to do something you would have to shout, making yourself heard over the general din several minutes before it was really necessary, and call him from one end of the line to another, or just shout even if you couldn't see him.

Eamonn was clearly not ambitious. He said he was just a small cog in the machine, and had no more power than we did. He supported us in the dispute, and agreed that the wages – including his – were abominable, and that UMEC was only interested in its profits. Like us, he knew all the ways the line could be run more efficiently, but he couldn't do anything about it. He had opted for an easy life, and his pay-off for not bossing us around was that we were very co-operative with him, and more or less ran the line ourselves.

Eamonn was in his early thirties, with a pale freckled complexion and red hair. He was married with two small children, and was clearly well cared for; he came in a clean ironed shirt every morning and was overfed. Of course he had staff status, and ate in the staff rather than the 'works' canteen. He didn't have to clock on, but signed his name in a book instead. He got longer holidays, sick pay, and earned more than us. He said he took home only £2 more than we did, but we discovered that the chargehands grossed £68, so he must have been taking home at least £50, which was over £10 more than us, although low for a man. He had to work overtime when the 'swing shift' was on, and some Saturday mornings. His bonus was based on our line's productivity. There was no formal training for the job – anyone could do it. The only qualification was being a man. Young boys were attached to a chargehand to learn the job, and it didn't take them very long.

Although the chargehands held rather a lowly position in the factory as a whole, it seemed high to us and their conditions bore no resemblance to ours. An efficient charge-hand might run about a lot but he also had time to sit down and do nothing, while shouting at you to get on with your work. Their pace of work wasn't dictated directly by the line speed and they had freedom to walk around. They had to see that all the components reached us in time, but that was nothing to having all your physical movements completely controlled by the line. When you sat at the top of the line and heard Eamonn chatting with the other chargehands about horses and football while you were killing yourself to keep up with the speed, their job seemed a real doddle with its higher pay, some authority, but not much responsibility. Many of the Irish women thought the Irish chargehands were a 'bit soft' – it wasn't 'a fit job for a man'; they would do better to work 'in the building' where the pay was better and they could be in the fresh air.

We were all on good terms with Eamonn; he never shouted at us or told us off. He just let you get on with your work, and turned a blind eye to eating and reading at the wrong times. He warned me if the 'suits' were approaching while I was reading the paper. But his reluctance to exert authority was two-faced: when things got too much, he couldn't cope with the lack of discipline, and went straight to the supervisor. It was Eamonn who had Josey more or less sacked when he should have sorted her out himself. She was doing the boring subassembly job, making up cases from two components for Grace to put the basic mechanism in. She was fed up and had been chicken-clucking very loud since early morning; from time to time she stopped working so Grace was running out of cases. In the afternoon, Josey was getting on with her work very slowly, when Grace complained to Eamonn so that he'd make her hurry up. Instead of telling her off or threatening with the supervisor, he marched her straight off to the supervisor's box. The supervisor told her she was paid 'to do as you're told', and gave her the choice of 'behaving or signing the form'. She didn't know what the form was, and acted proud and huffy. She told him to 'hand over the form, duckie', which was unheard of impudence from an 18-year-old girl to the big supervisor. Anyway she signed the form and left that day. It was despicable; Eamonn should never have let it get to that stage, and the supervisor should only have given her a warning as it was her first visit 'to the box'. In the event, she was forced to leave 'voluntarily'. Since she hadn't been officially sacked, she wouldn't be able to claim dole for six weeks. The shop steward wouldn't take it up because Josey signed the form 'of her own free will'. Josey just joked about it, but I was really disgusted that it happened so quickly and that a young girl with no knowledge of what she was formally entitled to could be clobbered just for refusing to obey the discipline of the line. That episode lost Eamonn quite a lot of support, though we didn't discuss it in front of him. In ones and twos we agreed that you couldn't trust him, that he was two-faced.

Above the chargehands was the section supervisor, a sort of deputy supervisor. He took over the line when the charge-hand was away, and dealt with technical problems and queries about pay and the bonus. Ours, called Reg, knew a lot more about the processes than Eamonn, and I think he was supposed to ensure that all the lines ran smoothly and co-ordinate which line did which set. Reg was white and English, as were most men from this level upwards. He'd been there twenty-five years and had received his gold watch; he was about fifty, very active and efficient, constantly running about the place sorting out problems. He looked like one of those white toy dogs with a mechanical wagging tail, and he walked bent forwards, with white hair on the sides of his head combed backwards, and a fag end always sticking out of his mouth. He followed the supervisor like an obedient dog. Reg was a real 'sneak', on management's side, and he tried to cool out any problem by fobbing off the women, saying he would sort it out and then disappearing for the rest of the day. We were supposed to complain to him about problems before calling the shop steward. If you slowed down or threatened not to work unless he dealt with your complaint, he'd always mention the bonus. 'It's only you girls who'll suffer because you'll lose your bonus.' It was a way of setting the women against each other, by telling them you were losing them their bonus. It worked with Nora, who got annoyed if you slowed down, but most women had no respect for the bonus in any case. When I was given the torque-checking job permanently, he made a big fuss about the responsibility and the extra 2p an hour I would be earning. If I was good at it, he said, I might even be 'put forward' to become a reject operator. He made out that would be a big promotion and mean more money, although it was only an extra 2p an hour. He was always trying to break up the line into smaller groups so as to divide and rule better.

When I made fun of the extra money and said it would only amount to about 50p a week after deductions and wasn't worth mentioning, he didn't have anything to say.

Reg himself did a lot of grafting. The place wouldn't have managed so well without him. He had a teasing relation with the women, who were fond of him as well as being suspicious. He often played the fool and sat down with us at break-time and tried to pinch our food, or got people to bring in pieces of homemade cake for him. He was only friendly so he could find out what we were thinking and play on any hostilities. When he knew I was interested in how things worked, he always took time to come and explain to me how they did safety checks (for instance on the radioactive airspray), what cars the different sets were for, and what the new designs and changes in technology were to be. He also got me some washers to mend my bike, so was quite helpful. He only shouted at us in fun.

I had a constant battle with Reg over the fan in front of me which didn't work. I would call him over to complain, saying I wouldn't do any more work till it was repaired. Usually he promised to do something about it, then vanished. One morning when it was baking, already $76°F$ at 8 o'clock, I decided to sort it out myself and climbed onto the line to readjust the fan. Both Reg and the supervisor rapidly appeared from nowhere, shrieking at me to get down; they would be responsible for industrial injury if I fell off. This seemed to be their only concern, because still nothing was done. After that I decided to increase my attack and called Reg several times an hour whenever I saw him. In the end, the fan conked out completely and I resorted to using a Chinese paper fan making sure to fan myself whenever he was around. He told me they were taking the fans down anyway, 'because you don't need them, so there's no point mending them'. He maintained that two extractor fans high up near the ceiling, and which had never been switched on all the time I was there, were 'quite sufficient for the whole shopfloor'. I didn't know whether or not he was joking. When I left I told him I'd given 'lack of co-operation by section supervisor over the fan' as my reason for leaving.

Above Reg were the supervisors, only two for the whole

shop, each in charge of five or six lines. They lived in the
'boxes' and spent a lot of time on the phone, running round
telling the chargehands what to do, and generally sorting out
crises and personnel problems. Some of these tasks were very
mundane, like coming over to check whether you really
were at work if you had forgotten to clock your card. You
had to get their signature for a 'pass-out' to go to the first aid
or wages office or if you wanted to leave the factory before
the right time.

Arthur Drury, our supervisor, was quite easy-going. He'd
also been at UMEC for twenty-five years, though he was only
in his forties. He had worked his way up and Arlene and
Alice had had him as a chargehand years ago. He was rather
paternalistic, but well meaning, and spoke to you as if you
were three years old and a bit dim. He had a nervous laugh
and was rumoured to suffer from 'nerve trouble' ('watch him
scratching his bum all the time'). He was a weak character,
but kindly and less sneaky than Reg. When he interviewed
me for the job, he took great pains to tell me that I was just
'the sort of person we love to employ'. He thought teacher
unemployment was a great pity, and hoped I wouldn't be
too bored with the work. Apart from hiring and firing, his
work was mostly administrative. He was told what sets were
to be assembled and how many, and he passed on the orders
to the chargehands. If there were technical hitches he'd call
the engineers. Both supervisors seemed to live in the place;
even when I arrived very early in the morning like 7.10,
Arthur was there.

The other supervisor was in charge of the Mini line and
the lines making UMOs for lorries. He was much stricter and
delighted in telling off 'his girls'. He was of Irish origin,
called Sean Cooney, and the women said that he was really
a nothing, 'straight off a potato field', and that was why he
was so bossy; once he'd been given a little power, he thought
he owned the place and had to show who was in charge.

We had little contact with him, apart from hearing how
mean he was, until our line was moved right next to his
'box', while our old line was converted for the new Continental
sets. We were in between him and 'his girls', but luckily he
didn't become our supervisor. He had sent women 'upstairs'

for serious warnings for things we did all the time, and sent new girls for a warning if they couldn't keep up with the speed. When Geraldine hadn't been able to keep up with the line, Rosemary got her to hand in her notice before he could carry out his threat to send her for a warning. She'd only been there a few weeks, and shouldn't have been expected to keep up with a new job all on her own. Doreen came during her tea-break to tell us what was going on, and Rosemary fumed over to 'give out' to him in defence of her younger sister.

If Sean Cooney caught 'his girls' eating outside of the one official tea-break, or saw any reading matter on their benches, they were in for it straight away. He maintained strict control over the card-clocking when it was time to go home, and didn't allow 'his girls' even to approach the clock until 4.15, yet that was when they were actually supposed to start stamping their cards. He had to sit and watch our line eating hard-boiled eggs, ham rolls, bars of chocolate, and reading the paper at all sorts of odd times, and he couldn't do a thing about it. Once he couldn't resist telling Eamonn that Maureen, who was doing the lugs next to me, was eating a doughnut at 2.50 in the afternoon, which really wasn't allowed. He watched the jam trickling onto the bench with a very pained expression on his face.

Soon after we were put next to his lines, he managed to rearrange all his skips, boxes and store cupboards and so build a big wall between our line and his; this meant we couldn't talk to 'his girls' while we were working. But it also meant he couldn't see them properly either. Everyone hated him, even the kindliest women.

When our line was moved we had to clock on 'his clock'. One petty incident showed to what lengths he would go to maintain his authority. There was always an issue of how early we could start queueing at the clock at the end of the afternoon. It was supposed to be a couple of minutes before 4.15, but we usually inched slowly towards it from about 4.11, making sure Arthur Drury wasn't looking. You couldn't clock before the siren sounded at 4.15 or you'd be docked money. There were at least fifty of us on Sean Cooney's clock so the last one couldn't clock out until about 4.25.

The minutes counted because they didn't pay you if you arrived early and you weren't paid for a second after 4.15 – you wanted to make sure to clock as close to 4.15 as possible, and run 'up the road' and out of the gates as fast as you could. There was always a mad rush to clock; if you didn't queue up and get your card out of its slot beforehand, everyone pushed in, pandemonium ensued and the whole thing took much longer. So our line carried on as before and queued up soon after 4.10. We couldn't start any earlier because the last tray came at about ten past, and then we had to tidy our benches and clear up, before getting our coats. Our line stood in front, by the clock, and 'his girls', who usually waited a bit, followed right behind us.

Sean Cooney was furious. He said he wouldn't have us on 'his clock', we were a bad influence and he would send the whole lot of us 'upstairs' for a warning the next day. He called over Arthur Drury who made a big show of being ashamed of us, and told us this was 'the thin end of the wedge; it will soon be ten past, then five past'. He told us that in future we were to go back and stand by our benches after we had put on our coats until the siren went, and only then queue up at the clock. I pointed out that we couldn't possibly queue before eleven minutes past because we were still working, and another woman asked if he wanted a stampede at 4.15 with everyone falling over each other and crashing into the skips in their haste to get to the clock. He got very flustered and said it was all right to queue just 'a couple of minutes' before 4.15, and shook with anger when we said that was all we were doing.

Of course we weren't sent 'upstairs' the next morning, and we resolved to carry on as usual. Carol came over and gave Sean Cooney a speech about 'custom and practice'. But the day after, our line was moved to a third clock, a decrepit old thing right at the back of the shop. We had to kick and bang it to stamp the cards at all, and it was much further to run to the factory gates. But at least Sean Cooney had removed our influence from his section.

On a later occasion, both supervisors decided on a concerted attempt to stop us queueing before the statutory time. They posted chargehands in front of the clocks to stop us getting anywhere near them. We got over that one though. Joyce, our electrical checker, was much bigger than the chargehand. She marched straight up to him and started to pull down his trousers. We knew pregnant women were allowed to stand at the front of the queue, so Maureen, who really was seven months pregnant, barged in between him and the clock, and the rest of us followed saying we were all pregnant. The packer at the end of our line who was rather fat, lifted up her skirt to show him her stomach and we all laughed at him.

They were pretty trivial incidents but they showed what the supervisors would do to extend their control, even though there would be no gain in production. It was like being back at school. If we hadn't resisted they would have tried on even more and attempted to frighten the women into obeying their every command for fear of a warning or dismissal. Like all factories, rights over time were one of the main bones of contention between us and the supervisors. They tried to get as much work out of us as possible in the time the firm was paying us for, and we wanted to make sure they didn't get away with one second extra.

The battles over the clock also showed how sexist their authority was. There was no way Sean Cooney could have told men to go and stand at their benches – men would have taken no notice. The tone of voice was of a man in authority talking down to a woman in a much lower position, as if we were a bit stupid for not realising what the punishment would be if our misdemeanours were reported to management. Calling us 'girls' and 'dear' created an air of paternalism that would never have been possible with men.

During the spring, the supervisors went on a work to rule and overtime ban, in support of a wage claim. Management suspended them and they stopped work altogether for a couple of days until it was settled. As the supervisors refused to order components, some of the assembly lines had to stop working when supplies ran out. So we lost our bonus because of them, and would have been laid off altogether if their dispute had carried on. We were put out by it; it was one thing to decide to forgo our bonus for our own reasons, but quite another to have it removed because of them. They acted as if their dispute didn't affect us at all, and was their own private affair, and Sean Cooney just sat in his 'box' all day grinning. It was the opposite when we were in dispute and suspended. Then the supervisors and the chargehands were both paid normally, so it was we who lost out on both occasions. The women on the Mini line suspected Sean Cooney had hidden the components because they had to stop work for lack of materials and were threatened with lay off and no pay at all; but when the supervisors' claim was settled, the materials appeared within minutes and so they must have been on the shopfloor all the time.

It wouldn't have occurred to us to support the supervisors in their action; their pay was so much higher than ours in the first place and their conditions of work so much better. With their power over us, they seemed closer to management than to the shopfloor. How hard they worked depended on how much administration was needed to keep production at the right speed. They weren't physically controlled by the assembly line at all. It seemed inconceivable that they would support any claim of ours either; they benefited directly from keeping the women obedient to the line.

We had no reason to talk to any men higher than our supervisors. They were in charge of us; if the managers wanted to tick us off or the engineers tell us to handle the jig differently, they had to go through the supervisor. But we had most contact with the chargehands, and were friendliest with the labourers.

All sorts of other men came and went in the main assembly in addition to the production workers, but they didn't impinge on us directly. For a long time they all looked the same to me except for their clothes; some wore overalls, others trousers and jackets, and the rest were in suits. This coincided fairly rigidly with ethnic origin: black and Asian men in overalls, English men in suits, and Irish men in trousers and jackets. It indicated how high up they were. Men in overalls were obviously manual workers while the suits were engineers or managers.

The production of UMOs appeared to require a whole host of workers other than those who ran and worked the assembly lines; people to set up the lines, time the jobs, design the layout, ensure the supply of components, check the quality of the product, oversee the transport of UMOs out of the factory, and many others. Each task was the responsibility of a particular grade of worker specialised in that one area. Some grades seemed to mirror the production workers with their own equivalents of chargehand and supervisor, but others had a less obvious ladder of promotion. We considered all men as belonging to one large group but the division of labour in fact separated them into various grades and skills and levels within the grades.

We saw most of the quality controllers and progress chasers. At the lowest levels of quality control there were even some women, as well as young men of Asian descent, but they had different tasks. The women sat at the end of the lines, and spot checked for correct calibration and other possible faults, and they drew the chargehands' attention to rejects. They were practically all Irish and had friends on the line whom they sat with at tea-time. Daphne was friendly with the young Irish quality control woman who sometimes sat on our line. The lowest male grade, on the other hand, walked up the line, checking the UMO as each operator finished her work on it, and collected the fault sheets from the torque checker and electrical checker. They were supposed to see that not too many UMOs with the same fault were built up and sent along the line, for instance transistors with bent pins, or covers with oil smudges inside. There weren't many of them; one was a young man of Asian origin, already married at seventeen and very full of himself. He thought himself vastly superior to us. Then there was a Greek man who looked three-quarters asleep the whole time. They had nothing to do but walk along the line every couple of hours doing their checks.

The next level of quality control were mostly physically disabled white English men. They took a sample of finished UMOs from the end of the line and wheeled them off to dismantle entirely. If they found a fault that could be pinned down to you, like consistently leaving out a washer from under a nut, you were in for trouble.

There were also quality controllers in charge of specific components, like the filters or basic mechanisms and the higher levels of these were 'quality engineers' as I was told. If Arlene had trouble with her filters, Max, a middle-aged man from Poland, came to examine them and send them back as rejects to France or Germany. He looked like an absent-minded professor and muttered to himself, but was friendly towards us and came over for philosophical chats with Arlene. Faults in the basic mechanism were a more serious matter, as they were the main part of the UMO. It was important not to build up many UMOs with faulty basic mechanisms as they would have to be dismantled completely. Flocks of engineers descended if something was wrong with them and sometimes the line was stopped, to everyone's relief.

Progress chasers also hovered around the lines. Although it was a clerical job they were all men and practically all Irish. The highest levels decided which sets were to be made up and when, and the lower ones were responsible for seeing we had enough of the various components. They came to the shopfloor to check the stocks of nuts and screws, modules or covers. They seemed to be the same sort of level as the chargehands whom they spoke to as equals. They were mostly tweed-jacketed and the younger ones even wore jeans. One of the engineers who spoke to me was scathing about the progress chasers implying theirs wasn't a 'real' job and that they were a 'breed of cheats and liars'. They seemed quite human to the rest of us. He thought they had no skill, but were trumped-up pen pushers who conned the chargehands into thinking they knew nothing would run out when really they hadn't a clue what was in the stores. If the line had to stop because we ran out of parts, it was their responsibility, he said, but you wouldn't often see progress chasers carrying skips themselves. We laughed at his criticisms because nobody carried skips on the shopfloor, they were much too heavy and were brought on mechanical trolleys or fork-lift trucks. Anyway the chasers did run about a lot. They were in a different union from us but were quite supportive during the dispute, blacking a lot of components. They had several disputes of their own, also about wages, and our shop stewards treated them as potential allies, like the chargehands, and unlike the other groups.

I had problems with one of the progress chasers, a trendy chap called Mike who wore a velvet jacket and Indian silk scarf and so stuck out rather from the rest of the men. It started with him throwing sweets and sticks of Juicy Fruit chewing gum onto my bench as he walked past. Then he started coming over to chat me up, finding excuses to check on the washers near me several times a day. Once he started talking, he never stopped no matter how busy I was, and as I was stuck to the line and he was mobile there was no getting away from him. I had no interest in him but all the others teased me about 'my boyfriend'. Of course Daphne spotted him approaching from miles away and announced to the whole line that he was coming, so they all watched. Even Carol came over from three lines away to ask 'how's your boyfriend?' Some days when I was at the top of the line doing modules for the Princess, I made Eamonn promise to get talking to Mike, and keep him away from me. I thought he was gay, but when I told the others that, Eamonn got worried about talking to him himself, and the women took it the wrong way, and started gossiping that he was 'bent'. Just coping with him would have been all right, it was the teasing that got me down. In the end he left because the pay was so low, and got a job as a milkman. After that he used to chase me down the High Street on his milkfloat but my bike was too fast for him.

The different types of engineers took some sorting out. From their dress and manner some were clearly graduates, but others seemed to have worked their way up. They were all dressed formally and none wore jeans. They were all English born except Mr Ghandi, who was Indian and said to be very clever with 'lots of letters after his name'. He was exceedingly elegant, and wore a different suit every day of the week. There was considerable interest in how many shirts and ties he had; Daphne thought she had worked out the right number. He was the only engineer who spoke to us and was quite friendly. I wondered whether that was because he was an immigrant, too. In any case, he didn't talk down to us, but as he was involved in setting up the new Continental line it was important that he had our co-operation in telling him about problems with the new jigs and machinery.

Some of younger engineers were quite chatty, but also only because they wanted information about the components. The women would never initiate a conversation with them – we waited until spoken to. There was also a horrible middle-aged 'chief quality engineer' who worked with Mr Ghandi. He could tell I was different from the other women because I read the *Guardian* and he wouldn't leave me alone. He tried to find out who I was and kept making silly comments, like what a left-wing paper the *Guardian* was and that I must fancy myself as an intellectual. He wanted to provoke me into an argument and I really had to control myself because I'd have been out on my ear if I'd had a go at him. Anna started folding her 'big' paper very noisily when he approached to divert his attention, and Mr Ghandi was embarrassed at his bullying. I tried to ignore him completely. Eventually when I revealed that I had been a teacher, he changed his tune and became smarmy, over-concerned to find me 'a more interesting job'. I took the opportunity to pump him for information about the different sorts of engineers and it was he who railed against the progress chasers. He himself had been at UMEC for twenty-seven years, having started at fourteen as a 'shop boy' in the days when men worked on the line; he had worked his way up, acquiring qualifications *en route*. He said there were quality, production and production development engineers and those who came round the new lines would be mostly production development. Many engineers were taken on at eighteen, and like him did sandwich courses and degrees at the firm's expense.

The engineers seemed quite different from the shopfloor workers – professionals, concerned about their work and the running of the line, but uninterested in the line workers over whom they had no authority. Breakdowns which came as a relief to us appeared to be an irritating interruption to them, and they reacted to our dispute as a nuisance. The lower–level engineers seemed similar to the supervisors, but younger and read the *Sun* and *Mirror*, while the older higher-ups seemed on fairly equal terms with the managers and carried 'big' papers. Overall I suspect they were closest to the supervisors in outlook and interests. Their experience was so remote from ours that they wouldn't have been interested in any problem of ours, nor us in theirs.

Time-study were the only other men we saw regularly on the shopfloor. They timed new jobs with a stopwatch, and retimed old ones that we complained about; they stood for hours, literally, retiming the same movements over and over again. We had a general understanding that you 'took your time' when they were timing you; if you had any subassembling you did it for each UMO at a time, rather than in a whole batch as usual. When Arlene's filter job was retimed and she did it according to the rules, just making up two at a time, she created a massive pile up of trays like we'd never seen before. The time-study men were definitely 'on the other side', working out the layouts and time sheets for each job and set; we took it for granted that they were 'for the firm', trying to cram as much into each operator's job as they possibly could. They were mostly in their twenties, English and informally dressed, and some of them tried, unsuccessfully, to be matey with us. We ignored them.

Above all these men were the managers. Those who visited the main assembly seemed to be directly in charge of the supervisors, and we were very wary of them as they were such 'big shots'. It seemed that in the past there was a ladder of promotion from supervision to management; the man who used to be over our two supervisors graduated from 'white coat' to 'suit'. He moved off the shopfloor, presumably into an office, and from then on hung around with the other 'suits'. It must have taken him twenty-five to thirty years to get from dogsbody on the shopfloor to that position, but I doubt whether that sort of promotion still exists for the younger men, as many of the managers must have acquired professional qualifications before UMEC took them on.

Two managers came round almost daily, whom I christened Tweedledum and Tweedledee. Tweedledum had cigarette-stained yellow hair, and always wore the same green suit, prompting comments about dirty clothes. He was healthy-looking and fat, but had a glass eye that always seemed to be staring at you. Tweedledee was small and thin, and had cigarette-stained hair, and his nose was very red-veined. If you hadn't heard his upper-class voice you could have mistaken him for a worker, he looked so pale and thin. They always walked together along the lines and stopped to chat with the supervisors, though Arthur Drury seemed nervous of them. When they were on the prowl you'd have to hide all sandwiches and newspapers, and make yourself very busy. When they came to wish the supervisors and chargehands 'Merry Christmas' they made a feeble attempt to include us in the greetings, although they never even acknowledged our existence at any other time. They stood at the top of the line and repeated 'Merry Christmas' down the line, as if to thin air, not addressing anyone in particular.

Tweedledum, Tweedledee and the other managers seemed like cardboard characters, and we thought them rude and bad mannered. Even if they stopped right by you or took the UMO out of your hand, they acted as if you weren't there. If they went through the heavy rubberised swing doors into the main assembly in front of you, they let them swing back on you, which no worker would ever do. Any of us would hold the door open for the next person automatically, even if it was management. They had so little respect for the workers that they couldn't even admit we existed.

Chapter Six
The dictatorship of production

Speed up

Most of the women agreed that the pace of work had become faster over the years. The light was flashing quicker, more trays had to be done, but there was less work to be done on each UMO. They also claimed that the conveyor belt itself moved faster, and jobs which used to be done by two people had gradually been turned into one-person jobs. My torque-checking job used to be separate from putting on the covers, but these had been combined. They said the speed used to be like the 'lollipop' job, the lightest job on our line; this was still a two-person job and an informal battle was going on to stop them turning it into a one-person job. If Alice or Arlene was away, Eamonn would try and get one woman to make up covers for both the basic mechanism and transistors. If she did it he could claim it was a one-person job. They were always looking for ways to make you do more, like giving you labels to stick on, or diodes to make up, as well as your normal work.

The main change over the last ten years seemed to have been that the components arrived more fully assembled so there was less subassembly to be done on the line. Now you just attached the parts into the case and screwed them down, whereas in the past you would have had to assemble them first. On the older Mini and lorry lines there was still quite a lot of subassembly, but practically none on the new Continental line. Before preassembled cases were introduced, Grace and Arlene had had to solder metal cases; each operator had so many jobs to do that the light flashed only once every nine minutes, whereas now it went every one-and-a-half to two minutes. They hadn't automated the line at all, but must have introduced more modern methods at the stage of producing the components, so we were doing just final assembly. This of course meant more repetition, doing the same smaller job much more often.

When Arlene's filters started arriving already assembled, we thought it was because of her demanding the job to be retimed. More likely, the new design had been in the pipeline all along. The more modern sets were made of aluminium and had pre-cut slots – all we had to do was align these slots to fix the components together. But the older sets were made of steel and everything had to be firmly screwed down with washers and nuts. The Princess covers, which took one person to attach, and the 'lollipop' job for the Maxi, which took three operators to make up and attach covers, were good examples of the difference. My Princess covers must have been mass produced – I took them ready-made from their polythene bags and clipped them into place, whereas Alice and Arlene actually made up the Maxi covers from their numerous components. They seemed much sturdier, needless to say. On the Mini line, they had an ancient machine that looked like an oven; the covers had to go in there to be soldered when they'd been assembled, before they could be attached to the UMO. The woman making up the covers had rubber bands and two metal rings, as well as all the bits and pieces we had for the 'lollipops'. The rings had to be taken out of paper bags, and the nickel thoroughly cleaned before assembly.

In the specialist shop just off the main assembly there was no line. Each woman made up the whole UMO herself by hand. The basic mechanism already had a module and sprocket, and had been calibrated by another group of operators who sat all day doing just that. They assembled only specialist orders: Rover, Jaguar, Vanden Plas, Rolls Royce and sports cars. The assemblers sat surrounded on three sides by boxes and skips, piled high, containing all the components needed for making up the UMO. They couldn't talk to each other because of these boxes, and as there were only a few airguns, it was very quiet in there. But the atmosphere was frantic, as the target for reaching the individual bonus was so high. Each woman had to make up between 20 and 25 boxes a day, each with 5 or 6 UMOs, and had to keep up a terrific pace to achieve this. In money terms, their bonus was only the same as ours so the work hardly seemed worth it.

One day Maureen took me into the specialist shop to have my hand read but her friend, the fortune teller, was too busy to do it. It was 3.15 p.m. and she'd done only 17 out of her 22 boxes, so she was in a mad panic as there was only an hour till 'going home' time. She'd run out of transistors and was shouting to the chargehand for more. She couldn't do any work without them, and would lose her bonus for however long she was stopped. All the women were working very, very quickly, not looking up at all from their work as they talked to us.

When the Triumph Speke plant was on strike, some women from the specialist shop came to work on the lines and were faster than us. They picked up the jobs quickly even when they'd never done them before. I think the supervisors considered them 'better' workers than us, but we didn't envy them their work.

The components for the specialist shop sets must have been more preassembled than ours, as they used so little machinery, and we were able to attach most of the pieces to each other simply by hand. The general trend towards less subassembling on the line didn't make the work any easier, only more boring.

At the same time, some individual jobs were made harder but for different reasons. Daphne and Alice's transistors for instance became practically impossible to do in the time. They used to arrive from the factory in Scotland, laid out in trays of twenty. Daphne and Alice had to take these trays, which were ready to use, out of larger cardboard boxes containing several trays. All of a sudden this changed; now the transistors came individually packed in small cardboard boxes, in larger boxes of twenty. Each was firmly secured in its own box and its three little 'legs' stuck out through three holes in the bottom of the box. To stop them jiggling about each 'leg' was tightly screwed down to the base of the box with a metal ring. Now before they could start on their work, Daphne and Alice had to take three of the small cardboard boxes out of the larger boxes, unscrew the metal rings, remove the transistors from the small boxes and put them in the old trays which they had kept. The rings were so stiff that they often couldn't unscrew them and their fingers got red and sore. In the end Reg produced some pliers for them. The new system meant unscrewing nine metal rings for each UMO as there were three transistors for each. In addition the metal rings had to be put in another special box to go back to Scotland, and the small cardboard boxes had to be replaced in the larger box. Somehow space had to be made on the bench for all these extra boxes. Only after all this could they start on the UMO. As they had one to do every two minutes, you can imagine how much extra work it involved.

Both Daphne and Alice had been doing transistors for years and were very experienced, but they could only just keep up with these boxes. When Grace was 'up the wall' in front of them, it put them right out because their trays weren't coming at regular intervals, and it affected everyone else behind as well. It was important to have some transistors already laid out in the old trays so that when the trays of UMOs came at shorter intervals than two minutes, they wouldn't be slowed down by having to do all the unpackaging. Every spare second was taken up with unboxing the transistors and Alice even spent her tea-breaks doing them.

When Alice was off sick, I was put on the job. I'd done it before and could just keep up, but with the boxes I didn't have a chance. There wasn't a second to relax. It was one of those situations I had to work so fast I felt it was a strain on my heart. Eamonn and Sharon occasionally came over to unbox a few transistors for me, and Daphne gave me some of hers, otherwise I would have been completely 'up the wall'. So of course I complained to Reg that the job ought to be retimed. He said it was all on the layout. That was hard to believe, because it hadn't been retimed and the original job must have been on the layout. He brought the layout sheet, and read out 'unpacking the transistors' but of course that meant from the old boxes, not these new Russian eggs.

Nothing was done about it and no one said why the system had been changed. Before, there had been so many reject transistors with bent pins or ones that didn't work at all, that I imagine all the packaging was intended to prevent them being damaged *en route* from Scotland.

During the months I was at UMEC, the organisation of the work was changed in several ways. Taken together these added up to an attempt to cut down on costs, but at our expense. For example, when I started, the changeovers from one set to another were quite leisurely. We had a short break in between while Eamonn brought the new components, we cleaned our benches and got the jigs ready. I had to alter all the leads on the electrical machine and change the endpiece for checking torque. Then I got out different screws and sorted out the radioactive spray and all my boxes. All the sticks across the line had to be moved to our new positions. Within several months, the changeover times had become much shorter, and we carried straight on from one set to another without a gap. I would just be finishing my last UMO on the old set when the first tray with the new ones would arrive, before I had time to sort myself out, or deal with the returned rejects from the old set. We couldn't start the new set until all the rejects from the last had gone right off the line but now I had to let Sharon and Kathleen finish off the work on the rejects. I had to rush around even faster to get it all ready, usually getting 'up the wall' in the process. The first hour or so on a new set became a tremendous strain.

At the same time they started cutting down on breakdown times as well; before when a machine broke down, as Grace's often did, the line would be stopped or rather Nora was told to stop feeding the light, until the mechanic had come and mended it. The same happened if someone ran out of components, and we would get a few minutes' rest. With the change, though, they carried on feeding right through a breakdown. This of course created huge pile ups which we had almost to kill ourselves to get through when the machine was mended or new components had arrived. They only stopped feeding if it was absolutely necessary – a long breakdown or a huge pile up. Five minutes of breakdown would mean a pile up of three trays or six UMOs. This might not

sound much but it could put you out for a long time afterwards, because the work was so finely timed that you only
just had time to do the one tray in between the lights in any
case.

A new category of worker was introduced, called a 'material
feeder'. This was to be a lower grade than chargehand, and
the chargehands were upgraded to 'production supervisor'.
This was an attempt to subdivide the chargehands' work into
more menial and more skilled elements. The material feeders
were less skilled and lower paid and there were more of them,
while the production supervisor grade was reserved for fewer
people, the old chargehands who were informally promoted.
So you could see it as an attempt at 'deskilling'.

Several new lines were opened in the main assembly and
some were transferred from Assembly 2. Instead of employing more chargehands, the existing ones were each put in
charge of two or even three lines. They were supposed to
take more decisions, leaving the humping and carrying to
the material feeders. In theory the material feeders' only
responsibility was to keep the line fed with components,
make sure we didn't run out and take away empty boxes.
They weren't on the staff and were more like us. Of course
they were all men, and as befitted their lower status, nine
out of the eleven were foreign-born: a few Irish and the rest
European.

In practice the division between the two grades didn't
work out so neatly, as the material feeders tried to increase
their pay and get promoted. Really their job was that of a
deputy chargehand – they had to know all the jobs (in
theory, not how to do them in practice) and what could go
wrong with the line, so as to anticipate what materials were
needed and when. They were told the only difference between
them and chargehands was that they were not 'in charge of
the girls'. Even this wasn't strictly true, as Pete, the material
feeder for our line certainly tried to take charge of us.
Eamonn, on the other hand, was not responsible for two
lines, and became lazier and fatter.

Pete was a pleasant young chap from Belfast, aged twenty-
four, with long hair and a beard. He wore faded jeans and
cowboy boots, had hitched around Europe and America,

and was saving up to go to India. He'd done all sorts of jobs, and worked in a record shop just before coming to UMEC. Pete was easy to talk to, and openminded. At first he used to sit on the line to try and learn some of the jobs. Everyone found this amusing, and referred to him as 'one of the girls'. He treated us as equals, and talked quite openly about his pay, conditions of employment, and how he had got the job, and he repeated conversations he had with Arthur Drury to us. He sorted out the various lugs for Maureen when she was tired, and helped unpack Alice's transistors. I said to Arlene that he seemed nice enough, but she laughed – I should wait for two months, because he would be 'on the other side' by then. And this was in fact what happened.

It was obvious to Pete that he was doing a chargehand's job but for less pay. He wanted Arthur Drury to notice how much more efficient he was than Eamonn so he'd be able to argue for a pay rise. He became very bossy, and assumed an authority that he had no right to. He acted as if he was doing us a great favour whenever he brought components or took away boxes, and stood waiting for us to say 'please' and 'thank you'. We bawled him out because it was his job to fetch and carry, and no one said please and thank you to us every time a tray came down the line.

Eamonn was away for a week and Pete got his chance. If any of our trays piled up, he said that we were trying to see 'what we could get away with' while he was on his own, and called over Arthur Drury to show he was tough. When Sharon asked him to stop the line, so we could get through a big pile up, his only comment was 'Sharon's trouble is she thinks she's a white coat', which just about summed up his new opinion of himself and us. He identified totally with his superior position even though he knew the only reason he had that job was because he was a man, and had been quite sympathetic about the work on the line when he started. He led the other material feeders in demanding a pay increase which they won. So the policy of deskilling seemed to backfire on the firm, with the material feeders now being paid only a few pounds less a week than production supervisors, and presumably in line for promotion to this position with its perks when they had gained a bit more experience.

Pete wasn't a nasty person, and certainly wouldn't have analysed the situation in terms of the firm's policies of employing less skilled workers. But the authority over us that went with his job seemed to lead him to identify, more or less naturally, with his position in the hierarchy, and to treat people both above and below from his particular rung. He lost a lot of popularity and we made fun of him, begging him exaggeratedly to fetch us components, to take him down a peg or two. We stopped exchanging sweets with him, and talked about him behind his back.

Putting two lines under one chargehand made them more flexible. Women could be transferred from one line to the other if people were away, or if more operators were needed for a particular set. The reject operators were sometimes moved to the other line just for parts of the day. Before Arthur Drury had come down all the lines first thing every morning to see who was away, and did a large-scale rearranging of operators between all the lines to fill the gaps.

Training new arrivals in most of the jobs on the line, as they did with me and some others, was another way of increasing flexibility. Most of the younger women, like Ann, Rosemary and Eileen, had only learned one or two jobs. We bore the cost of training and it was quite a strain as I discovered when I had to train a new girl in modules. I had to work extra fast to show her what to do, and then take over myself when the backlog of trays slowed down the women behind. Eamonn's two lines learned each other's sets, so they could be switched from one to another at a moment's notice. We were both working exclusively on Leyland sets, and our line came to do Allegro and Marina sets more regularly than before, and the other line learnt the Maxi, Princess and Mini Clubman.

Just before Christmas, Eamonn told us that the firm was introducing a productivity scheme. Soon the materials became shoddier and needed closer inspection. More reject components meant more work for us – the scratched silicones for the Princess module were just one example of this. So the scheme appeared to be self-financed by cutting back on materials, as well as electricity and heating. I don't know whether this worked out cheaper over all – from the line, it certainly didn't look like it. I suspected that the other changes we noticed, cutting down time lost on changeovers and breakdowns, and the materials feeders, were all part of this same scheme.

The three new lines that were set up must have helped the firm raise its profit margins. The only cost looked like the carpentry needed for the construction of the line, and the machinery, which in any case didn't look brand new. There was no additional overhead cost because more people now used the same space, heating, lighting and toilets.

The number of assemblers became less as women who left weren't replaced, so the lines were producing more with fewer operators and sometimes one woman came to do the job of two. Between September and Christmas our line lost three workers, yet we still churned out the same number of UMOs every day. UMEC was advertising for assemblers in shops as well as in the local papers and cinema, so this drop in numbers probably wasn't intentional. Many new women stayed only for a few days, finding the work worse than where they had been before, whether it was Victoria Trading Estate or the West of Ireland. Apart from a few school leavers, most of the new recruits were straight over from Ireland.

With fewer operators and the cheaper materials feeders, these new lines must have been quite an 'economical' expansion. The increased intensity of work for all of us raised productivity in the shop generally without adding to wages, and the use of cheaper components cut down on the cost of raw materials. We doubted that this would be reflected in the price they charged the customer for UMOs. Altogether the pace of work was increasing in small and subtle ways which it would have been difficult to oppose, except in a very organised way.

I thought the unions would take up these changes because they made such a difference to our conditions of work, but they didn't seem to bother about much other than wages. In any case the firm could argue that they weren't negotiable because it was up to them what work we did during the time they paid us. As Arlene said, you had to give them credit for getting us to work even harder, so the joke was really on us.

Their outlay didn't include the cost to us in extra work and tiredness that went with the productivity scheme. Now the pace was so fast that if you stopped to complain about it you had even more work to catch up with.

Control of the line

The women ran the line, but we were also just appendages to it. Its discipline was imposed automatically through the light, the conveyor belt and the bonus system. We just slotted in like cogs in a wheel. Every movement we made and every second of our time was controlled by the line; the charge-hands and supervisors didn't even have to tell us when to get on. They just made people like Josey obey if they wouldn't buckle under. You couldn't really oppose the organisation of the work because it operated mechanically. The only things you could challenge were the petty rules, or management's attempts to speed up the work. The bonus system and the line speed even led the women to discipline each other; getting 'up the wall' put out the person behind and we had informal arrangements to help avoid that. But these also ensured that we made up the right number of UMOs, so the supervisors' job was really done for them.

Although we were the only workers with practical experience of working on the line, our views were not taken into account. Changes were made, new designs and machinery introduced with no regard for us. The engineers never had to sit down and use most of their jigs and were often clueless as to how they worked in practice. Most of the women could have told them how the machinery could be made more comfortable, which jobs went best together, and how the line could work more efficiently. But no one ever asked us. If you pointed out why something didn't work to an engineer he looked at you as if you were a freak, or pretended he hadn't heard. One young engineer took about five minutes to show me how to move a cover for a new set two inches to the left to fit a valve in it. When I told him it couldn't be done like that because the cover was lying in a jig, blocking the hole for the valve, he stared at me as if I was mad. What he said just didn't make sense and I carried on doing the job by holding the cover upside down outside of the jig.

From the firm's point of view, our job was unskilled and purely manual. 'Anyone' could do it – it only required women's nimble fingers. We had to call a mechanic over for the tiniest fault, and the chargehands even changed the screwheads for the airguns, and endpieces for the calibrating and checking machines, when their lines switched to a new set. On our line, we did our own, and there was nothing to it. But that wasn't the point – we were paid to be operators, not mechanics or chargehands.

When new machinery was introduced, they didn't measure it for height, or work out where exactly it should be placed, but just plonked it down anywhere. Then you had to contort yourself to reach it. The new chairs were a case in point: when the new lines started up, a batch of new chairs arrived, the stacking sort with adjustable height. Even at their highest, they were much too low to reach the airguns comfortably, and we got dreadful neckache from straining forwards. We had to bring in our own cushions from home to make them bearable. The old chairs had very hard seats but were much higher and became like gold dust. We squabbled over them, and accused others of pinching 'ours'. We could see what was wrong with the new chairs even before they were unpacked; it would have been the most obvious thing in the world to get the measurements right before ordering them.

The saga of my 'flyover' showed how the supervisors only cared about the product. On our 'old' line there was an empty bench behind me, where I put the rejects for Sharon and Kathleen to collect. But the new line was shorter and there were no empty benches. Alice sat right behind me doing the lollipop job. So there was nowhere to put the rejects the first morning, and I called Eamonn over to tell him, but nothing happened. The rejects started piling up, and I put them on the side of the line. All the trays bumped into them, and got stuck across the line, so it was very inconvenient. Then I called Reg. He said there should be no rejects anyway and walked off, so I shouted after him that I'd just drop them on the floor in that case and we could all forget about them. He came back with a long spiel about how the new line was fourteen foot shorter than the old one, and had fewer benches, which anyone could see. I made a few suggestions about how to shift the benches round, but he took no notice. Eventually he summoned the carpenter to come and build me a 'flyover'.

This was to be like a small coffee table that would stand over the line, with its legs on either side of the line, and I would put the rejects on top of it. Eventually it arrived and was nailed down to the sides of the line. Somehow I now had to fish the UMO out from underneath it. The sides were much too low and the wood wasn't planed, so I had to squeeze my arm under the side and up again to get the UMO out of the tray, scratching my wrists in the process. There was hardly enough room for the tray to slide underneath it. I couldn't see across the line any more, or talk to anyone, and was all boxed in. It was in the wrong place anyway and much too big. The bench had to be moved forward when we did the next set so that I could reach the airgun, and then I had to turn right round and lean over backwards to reach the fly-over and my trays. It slowed me down a lot because I had to be very careful not to bash the UMOs into the flyover when I was getting them out of the tray. By the end of the after-noon my arms were bleeding.

The next day was the worst ever, and I went home in a terrible rage. The supervisor had tried to stop us queueing up at the clock, and had 'persuaded' Josey to resign. I'd also had a lot of bother with Sharon who kept querying my rejects. It started badly in the morning, because every single UMO had some fault – the covers were scratched, the sprockets were bent, the rotors weren't straight, or the filters had screws rattling inside them. It was quicker to mend some of these myself, than go through the whole procedure for putting out rejects, what with Sharon and the flyover. Arlene was 'up the wall' in front of me, which made my work harder, but when she tried to go faster she only got the screws stuck inside the filters so they too became rejects. And the stupid flyover was getting on my nerves. To save time, I sent on a couple of UMOs with faults, and Joyce came to tell me I must put out all bad work as rejects. Then Arthur Drury ticked me off for putting reject components in the ordinary rubbish bin instead of having a special reject bin for them. But there simply wasn't room for a reject bin as well as all the other boxes and the flyover.

By about 8.30 in the morning I was extremely hot and bothered, and kept breaking out in a hot sweat. I thought I couldn't carry on with it. I called Eamonn over and told him to get the carpenter to move the flyover. About half an hour later he said he'd called the carpenter, but thought he wouldn't be able to move it for about three months. I exploded, called Reg, and said I wasn't doing any more work till the flyover was changed. He started on one of his calming-down talks – 'now dear what's the matter', when he knew perfectly well what the matter was. I was determined to get the thing changed even if it meant letting all my trays pile up, and annoying all the other women by making a huge back-log; it would have been stupid to let them get away with it. Nothing happened until I mentioned to Reg that I was banging the UMOs into the flyover, as well as my wrists. Then he called the carpenter quick enough. Carpenter and mate arrived and I showed them where it should be planed down and where the legs should be, so that I could reach the trays.

Back it came in the afternoon, and in the meantime I had to clear a great pile up of trays with nowhere to put the rejects again. Eamonn and Reg stood around as they started to nail it down. I said there was no point doing that if the bench had to be moved backwards and forwards for the different sets, because it would be too far away from me and in the way of someone else. They started joking about 'women never knowing what they want and always changing their minds', so I invited them to sit down and do the job, because they'd soon see that the flyover had to be moveable. That started them off on 'you can tell she's a teacher, can't you?', so I couldn't win. In the end they left it not nailed down, laughing that I could change my mind as much as I liked about where I wanted it.

All the fuss and bother showed they would listen only if the product was in danger and, even so, they acted as if they were paying for the flyover out of their own pockets. After my success, Arlene was persuaded to complain about the filters, but many of the older women just 'made do' with very awkward jigs and machines. They sorted themselves out as best they could, to avoid trouble. The younger ones were more inclined to 'give out' with varying degrees of success. Rosemary was always complaining, and managed to get machines changed that other women had been using for years and couldn't be bothered to make a fuss over even when they were very uncomfortable. But as Rosemary said, UMEC would try and get away with anything, and unless you complained it would just get worse and worse. Organising the work better would have earned the firm a little good will and would probably have raised productivity – but you couldn't imagine them doing it.

The speed they ran the line was so fast that it was counter-productive – actually creating more work. The faster the line, the more rejects were made. Everyone knew this, but then we realised that the firm wanted to churn out as many UMOs as quickly as possible. When we were on go-slow and did half the number, there were virtually no rejects as we had time to do the job properly. At normal speed up to a quarter of them might be rejects. They could have had the line running slower and saved the two reject operators. But time-study must have calculated that it was cheaper for the firm to have more rejects and two women to mend them, than have a slower line with fewer operators, especially as the exhausting effect of the fast line wouldn't enter their arithmetic.

Doing time

It is impossible to put over in writing the speed of the line, the pace of work, and the fiddliness of the jobs we had to repeat all day long, as tray followed tray down the line. We were physically geared up, straining to get it done as fast as we could, and the atmosphere was frantic. Everything was rushed, work, breaks, drinking tea, reading the paper. We were so speedy that we rushed at everything, and the breaks were very short compared to the work time. At lunchtime we rushed to clock, ran to the canteen, or out shopping, and ran back again. There was no time to slow down or do anything at 'normal' pace. It took me hours to relax after work and stop feeling the line whirr through me. Until then I turned everything into mechanical operations to be done as fast as possible.

Working on the line changed the way you experienced time altogether. The minutes and hours went very slowly, but the days passed very quickly once they were over, and the weeks rushed by. Some days were even slower than others, and everyone agreed whether the morning was fast or slow, and whether the afternoon was faster or slower than the morning. We joked about how we were wishing our lives away, wishing it was 'going home time' or Friday afternoon.

In the morning, we were at it from 7.30 till 12. Our breaks were at 9.10, 9.50 and 11.10, so the earliest part was the worst. Between 9 and 10 wasn't too bad, but the stretch between 10 and 11.10 was very long. Lunchtime was from 12 to 12.45, then there was a five minute break at 2.30, and ten minutes at 3.10. The breaks at 9.50 and 2.30 were the only official ones for the whole factory. The others were unofficial ones for assembly line workers to go to the loo, and when the line was 'on relief' we didn't get proper breaks at all. The line was switched off only at 9.50 and 12 so the other breaks were very noisy.

The day seemed very long; 10 in the morning was like 2 in the afternoon had been to me before. The afternoon (that is, after 12.45), was called 'the evening'. By 2.30 you could see your way to the end of the evening, and after the last break at 3.10 there was only another hour to go. The stretches of nearly two hours without a rest were very exhausting, and the breaks seemed far too few.

You wanted to make sure to use the breaks for yourself, not to 'get down the wall' as some people did, or to unbox transistors like poor Alice. Most people had a routine for the break, exchanging the *Mirror* and *Sun* or going to chat with a friend. I came to guard my breaks jealously, and that's why Anna sometimes irritated me, intruding on my free time to grumble about the firm's profits when I wanted to read the paper in peace. Our co-operative flask filling saved us a few minutes. When I did them first thing in the morning we avoided the queues at the water-filling machine at 9.50, and could get our tea ready beforehand. I had the 11.10 break and lunchtime free because Rosemary refilled the flasks ready for Alice, Grace and me.

Many of the women stayed at their benches at lunchtime, eating their own sandwiches, or getting others to bring them back food from the canteen. I thought this was horrible at first, being stuck in the stuffy atmosphere all day. But in fact it gave you much more time than queueing up in the canteen. It meant you didn't go out all day. We never saw the daylight all winter and didn't know what the weather had been, as we arrived in the dark and went home in the dark.

Somehow the rituals made the day go faster, and they also divided up the week. Sharon and Kathleen coming round for orders from the canteen and coming back with the rolls gave a bit of interest early on. Everyone examined their roll for size, freshness and colour. You could have crusty or soft ones, but often you couldn't tell the difference between them.

Sometimes 7.30 to 9.10 seemed like several days in itself, and I would redivide it up by starting on my sandwiches (hidden under the torque checking machine) at 8 a.m. I would look at the clock when we'd already been working for ages, and find it was only 8.05, or, on very bad days, 7.50 – more than another whole hour to go to the first break. Then I redivided the time into half hours, and ten-minute periods to get through, and worked out how many UMOs I'd have done in ten minutes, twenty minutes and half an hour; then I thought about everyone from my previous life and whether they would have got up yet and when they would be leaving for work. It was the same every day after lunch – you'd have been working for what seemed like days and days, but it was only 1.20 and there was more than an hour to go to the next break.

Monday wasn't too bad as a day, but Tuesday was never-ending. Nothing happened on Tuesday, it wasn't a special day in any sense. At least Monday was the first day of the week, and we could catch up with the weekend news, and it seemed quite a long time since Friday. On Wednesday,

Eamonn came round with our bonus points for the previous week which would go into tomorrow's pay, so we were getting on for Thursday. The points gave us something to argue about, and we didn't hesitate to complain if they seemed too low. By Wednesday lunchtime, people would say half the week was over and we could see our way to Friday afternoon. Thursday could be a very long day as well, even though it was payday. The pay slips were brought round at about 9.30. We scrutinised them, compared each others, and generally assessed whether we'd been paid enough. If someone's deductions were wrong, the whole line knew after a few minutes, and that would give us a few minutes' interest. People often came at 9.50 to ask me to explain changes in the percentage bonus, or why their tax was different from the week before. The money itself came at 2.30. It was quite exciting, opening the envelope and checking that it was all there. Then many visitors came over with pools money for Arlene, and £1 notes for Grace. She ordered clothes from a mail-order catalogue for them on the never-never. If we received more money in a particular week, we'd discuss what to spend the extra on. Usually it went towards something like a pair of shoes that we hadn't had enough money for before. If we got less than expected, we were outraged, like when the supervisors were on work to rule and our bonus went down.

Friday was the beginning of the clocking week again. The week went from Friday to Thursday. You were paid a week in hand so if you were away on a Friday you wouldn't notice it in your pay packet the following week, but the one after that, when you'd already forgotten about being away. Then the small wages came as a big shock. Fridays could be very boring, too, but there was fish and chips for 12p to look forward to in the canteen. Everyone was sighing 'thank goodness, it's Friday', or 'only an afternoon left' or 'only two hours left'. The last tray was fed at 4.05 instead of 4.10, as we were supposed to clean our benches with spirit cleaner which Eamonn never ordered. Really this five minutes was nothing, but it seemed to make a great difference. If you managed to spin out the last break for an extra five minutes to nearly 3.25, there was only just over half an hour till finishing time, and then the weekend.

Even though the hours went so slowly, I couldn't remember everything that happened in the day. It seemed so long and so much had happened: discussions, breakdowns, small dramas, a union meeting perhaps. When you looked back on the week it seemed very long and eventful, yet I couldn't remember whether a particular incident happened this week or last. All the days were the same, but we made them significant by their small dramas. Unless I wrote down what happened in the evening, Monday, Tuesday and Wednesday were all jumbled together in my mind by the end of the week.

At Christmas there was a big question of whether we would have to stay right till the end of the afternoon on the last working day, Friday 23 December. A notice from management warned that we'd be docked all three days' holiday pay if we failed to work the day before or the day after the holiday. A lot of women said they were going to leave at lunchtime on the Friday, and it was a topic of discussion for days. I asked what had happened last year, whether they really had been docked the three days' pay, but no one could remember. At the time this seemed odd but I certainly wouldn't remember what happened in the end if I hadn't written it down, because from one Christmas to the next seemed like a million years.

Some of the older women trundled on all day, not particularly put out by the boredom. Anyway, there was nothing you could do about it. Arlene was deep in memories, and Alice sang hymns to herself. Grace always found something to laugh about, and Daphne watched everything that went on. Anna was absorbed in counting how many UMOs we got through and whether there were more or less than yesterday. But us younger ones were always moaning about how long the day was. We tried to rush to the loo in work-time to add a couple of extra minutes to the break. We were overjoyed if a light was missed or there was a breakdown. We had our tea prepared and the paper open on the right page so we wouldn't waste a split second of the break when the siren went. But we were so tensed up, we didn't relax at all. I tried to get to the middle page of the *Guardian* by lunchtime, just leaving the business news and television programmes for the afternoon. Then I scrounged other people's papers, or women's magazines and was enthralled by love stories that I'd normally sneer at.

If you had to miss your break to go to the wages office you resented it because it made the day feel so much longer.

Stoppages on the line were double-edged. We were glad to get the few minutes' rest, but it also cost us money. Nora and a couple of others were taken in by the bonus and wanted to do as much work as possible during the time, thinking they'd get more money at the end of the week. The older women were so used to working very fast that they found it quite hard to slow down when we were going slow and complained of being bored after a couple of weeks.

Sitting next to someone made the time pass more quickly. There was a good run of days when Rosemary, Eileen and I chatted and sang songs all day long. Rosemary told us about her family and what her brothers and sisters were doing, then she'd get Eileen to take over and tell her life story. We were all pleased when this happened because the time flew and the next break came quite soon. The conversation itself was almost secondary to passing the time. If you had a new woman sitting with you, or shared a job, that was great because you could sort out short rests between you and the day would pass more quickly because there was someone to talk to.

Sitting on your own, doing the build up or modules at the top of the line before the light, was the worst. I'd suddenly find myself humming a medley or I'd try to plan my weekend shopping, what I'd do in the evening or work out how much each line and each worker was paid per UMO. I thought of my friend in Manchester who worked in a factory where the women were on individual machines and had individual targets. The work there was simpler and more repetitive than ours; she told me that after they'd been chatting for a while, the women might announce to the person next to them that they were 'going inside' for a bit, meaning that they were going to daydream instead of chat. Ann at the top of the line must have been well and truly 'inside', as she didn't seem bored at all.

In the long run, you just had to put up with the tedium. Most of the women didn't expect work to be interesting. I made more of an issue about it because I wasn't used to it, but it was naïve on my part to ask them how they put up with it. Thinking about it all the time just made it worse.

As time was what we were paid for, we made a clear division between what was ours and what was theirs. Time was also discipline which the supervisors had to enforce. So the fights over clocking off were of more than symbolic importance – they were real attempts by them to encroach on our time and, by us, to resist such encroachments. Only the lowest grades actually had to queue up and stamp their cards three times a day, and UMEC was on to a good number in not letting us queue up till the actual clocking time. In other factories I'd heard of, clocking-off time was the time the last person clocked out. UMEC counted the minutes between 4.10 and 4.15 in lost UMOs, and every day the last few minutes before lunch and before the end of the afternoon were tense – as each side tried to see what it could get away with.

On the jobs before the light, where you could do a whole lot of modules or calibrating, and then take a rest, it was possible to spin out the breaks a bit. I tried to sneak out to lunch a few minutes early when I was doing modules, going through the loo and the machine shop to the canteen. But if you were caught out you were in for it, so you either had to hide or march about brazenly.

At first I thought it was ridiculous having to hide the newspaper if the managers came round during the break because surely what you did in the breaks was your own business. But Daphne put me right – if they were paying for the time, they could dictate what you did in it, and we were only supposed to go to the loo if it was an informal break.

The long day's work took a toll on the rest of your life. For a start, you were so tired and had so little spare time that you needed a stable domestic routine. Most of the time out of work was taken up with shopping, cooking, washing and cleaning, and you wanted to make sure to do these as quickly and efficiently as possible. The job only left time for basic living. I became quite obsessional about having a regular routine of shopping and laundretting. You couldn't let it pile up because then you'd have to do it all in one go and this would leave no free time at all.

The only relaxation for most of the women was watching

television, and going out on Saturday night. You were so exhausted that the evening was very short, because of going to bed early, and women with children had often been up since 5 a.m. An early night was 7 or 8 p.m., and 10 p.m. was considered late. Some of the younger girls managed a couple of late nights out, drinking or dancing, but then needed a very early night to recover. Once they reached twenty-two or twenty-three they couldn't even manage this. Saturday night was the only relaxed evening, when you weren't already dead beat from work, and wouldn't have to be up at the crack of dawn.

The work limited what you could do in your spare time, and completely determined the rest of your life. This was why Rosemary didn't like having too many friends, because of the time it took visiting them, and why most of the women thought it was no life for a youngster. It was easy to see the pressures forcing you into marriage, with stability, routine and no surprises; you could relax together in front of the box in the evening, and have a regular shopping, cleaning and going out routine. The women who shared bedsits, like Rosemary and Doreen, and Ann and Eileen, had such an organised domestic life that they would appear almost middle-aged in comparison with students of the same age.

The work changed my life completely. It was impossible to go on seeing all my friends, even those I was particularly close to, because physically I just wasn't up to it. I never went to visit them during the week, they had to come to me because I would have to go to bed so early; I always resisted going out to a meal and the cinema because of time, money and tiredness.

Physical survival

The speed of the line affected your whole body. Constant physcial pressure for eight hours left you tensed up. We all felt the same. I don't know whether assembly line workers suffer from stress diseases more than other types of worker, but it wouldn't surprise me. Arlene had recently started seeing 'a butterfly' in front of her eyes and the doctor said she had high blood pressure. Many women were taking

Valium and Librium for 'nerve trouble'. They all looked older than their age, pale, tired and drawn. They thought I was about eight years younger than I was and I thought them ten years older. Even the 20-year-olds had deep lines round their eyes.

Everyone complained about being 'jaded'. Getting up at 6.30, and working virtually non-stop from 7.30 knocked you out; you had to go to bed early not only to recover but also to be able to get up so early again. If you were off for a day, it was generally acknowledged you'd 'slept in' because you were too exhausted. You needed to take a day off now and then just to catch up on sleep. I used to think it was a waste of time to take a day off work just to sleep until I found you really needed to. Some of the women 'slept in' regularly, about once every two weeks, so the absenteeism rate must have been quite high.

My diary was full of days when I was 'bursting inside', 'gone over my physical limit', 'whirring', or had 'pains in the chest and felt faint'. It must be bad for the heart to push yourself so hard, and work at a pace much faster than is normal for the body.

It certainly took years off their lives. Apart from looking worn out, they thought fifty was old and didn't expect to live much after sixty or retirement age. That was realistic statistically, given that manual workers have a much lower life expectancy than professional workers. The two labourers who died while I was there were just under sixty, and three other men were said to have dropped dead from heart attacks on the shopfloor during the past year. On my last day, one of the progress chasers, in his mid-forties, had a heart attack. Alice thought the fact it was only men who dropped dead at work proved that 'we women are much stronger'. But the older women did look really haggard and some had difficulty keeping up with the speed.

You also suffered from various aches and pains. Sitting in the same position all day was almost unbearable – it made me feel like a stiff slug that couldn't even stretch. Backache and neckache were common, and excruciatingly painful. During the first few weeks screwing down resisters on the Maxi, I was in agony because of the way I had to strain forward to hold the airgun. The others had all been through it themselves when they started. Arlene's backache was so bad, she had paid £20 to the doctor for painkilling injections so that she could carry on working. If the chairs had been the right height and the jigs the right distance away, most of this would have been avoided. If we'd had time to stretch and walk about it wouldn't have been so bad, but the pace made it worse because you had to tense yourself up to work as fast as you could.

The women who did close work – the build up, calibrating, torque checking – complained of eye strain. When I checked for torque, the UMO was only about 9 inches from my eyes, and it was a strain to focus so close. The glaring lights and general tiredness made it worse. I'd never heard people complaining of 'sore eyes' before, nor had I ever suffered from eye strain. Rosemary had recently got glasses, as had several others and there was a general recognition that many of the jobs ruined your eyes. I began to suffer from eye ache and twitching eyes for the first time and couldn't wear contact lenses because my eyes were too tired, and it was too dirty to clean them properly. From the speed at which my eyes deteriorated, I could imagine going blind, though I doubt that this ever happened.

When I was interviewed for the job, they asked if I suffered from period pains, varicose veins or eye strain. Now I know why – you'd get them at UMEC even if you never had them before. Most of the younger women had bad period pains, made worse by sitting in the same position all day with no exercise. Rather than go home and lose money, they dosed themselves up with large quantities of painkillers. One morning, Maureen was rushed off to hospital, thinking she was in labour. It was a false alarm but the doctors said she should be moving about because the baby would get stuck in the wrong position if she sat in the same position all day. It's head was stuck against her ribs, which was very painful. But the only job where she could move around would have been packing, and that was far too heavy work, so she had to stay where she was or leave.

Some women contracted dermatitis from the grease they used in the build up, and you were more likely to get it if you worked at the top of the line. Carol, the shop steward, had it and was given some cream in first aid.

The ordinary air sprays for removing dust from the transistors were probably harmless, but their noise was irritating. You had to hold them across your lap, and sprayed youself in the stomach or face as well as the UMO. Everyone was wary of the radioactive sprays, and Arlene said she got stomach ache from it. Eamonn wouldn't come near mine. It was supposed to be set at a pressure of 20lb. but that didn't produce a strong enough jet, so we set it at 40lb. One day I felt quite sick and dizzy from it and called Reg over – we discovered that by mistake it has been set nearer 60lb. After that I decided to investigate it, and got in contact with the Work Hazards group of BSSRS (British Society for Social Responsibility in Science). From what they discovered, the spray should have been quite safe unless there was an oil leak, but I doubt whether you were supposed to inhale it all day.

The shopfloor was hardly ever swept, and was very cluttered. The toilets were revolting, although renovations were promised; there were no locks on the door, often no toilet roll, sometimes no light, and they were generally dirty and unhygienic. The fans were so ineffective that the air was always hot and stale. There seemed to be no circulation of air apart from holes in the glass roof that also let in the rain, and virtually no extraction of stale air, despite the fact that another UMEC firm manufactures industrial fans and air conditioners. The fire exit was often obscured by cardboard boxes and we never had a fire drill in seven months. The fire alarm went off twice, once because of a real fire, only small, in the machine shop. The supervisors sat as if deaf while the bells went on ringing. We joked that they'd rather let us burn to death than lose one minute's production, or they might take the UMOs out and leave us there.

If you felt ill, there wasn't much point going to the first aid because they dished out two Panadol tablets whatever your complaint. But they did bandage up my hand so the wound from the module machine looked more impressive than it was. No one trusted the nurses because we thought their job was to send us back to work; at Christmas one young Irish woman went to them feeling very ill with a splitting headache, and they sent her back to work with two Panadol tablets. In fact she had meningitis, but by the time it

was diagnosed it was too late. She died over the holiday. I'm
not suggesting that it was the first aid's fault, but we didn't
expect them to treat our aches and pains very seriously.

Working there made life a real battle for survival. All the
women were health-conscious, and, like Arlene, thought
nothing of paying for private medical treatment or drugs.
Grace was always saying that 'your health is all that you've
got'; you must look after it because no one else would, and
if it meant paying, it was just too bad. The West Indian
women, particularly, went to private doctors, and also paid
for private medical certificates. They thought the treatment
they'd get on the National Health Service was rubbish and
they'd have to wait such a long time for it that it was cheaper
to pay in the long run because they wouldn't miss so many
days off work.

Most of them were so unfit they got out of breath running
for the bus. But you had neither time nor energy for proper
exercise. From the dirty, noisy and exhausting factory
exercising to keep fit and not wearing make-up seemed like
middle-class fads. If you looked old before your time, came
home sweaty and dirty, and were lined and pale, the 'natural
look' held no attraction for you – it seemed more sensible
to cover the lines and 'improve' your colour with make-up.
We sprayed each other with eau de cologne several times a
day to smother the oily smell of the factory. If you have a
job that lets you sleep enough it's easy to view other women
who wear make-up as being conned by the media, and treat-
ing themselves as sex objects, but I came to realise it wasn't
nearly as simple as that.

The women on my line had a quite different attitude to
thinness and fatness from the one I was used to. Most were
quite big, ate a lot and seemed impervious to fashion magazines
wanting them to be thin. You had to eat a lot to keep up
your strength for the work, but it wasn't just that. They
equated being thin with being weak, and vice versa, so big
was healthy. Really it was the worst of all worlds, being big,
physically tired out but unexercised. I took it as an insult
when Grace said I was putting on weight, but she meant it
as a compliment – I would now be stronger.

Food was one of our main interests in life but always in

relation to health – what was best for replacing the calories we'd burned up, and what would help to keep us going. The women spent a large proportion of their wages on food, and much of it went on big slabs of meat, like steak, chops or joints. They didn't have time to cook meals that took longer, but used cheaper cuts. The West Indian women were particularly concerned about eating enough fresh fruit and vegetables. They brought in apples, oranges and grapefruit for the tea-breaks and Arlene often had an avocado pear and a banana for her lunch, but she made sure to have meat at night.

Each ethnic group was pretty chauvinist about the others' eating habits. The West Indians thought the Irish diet was unhealthy and made them fat and flabby – they should eat more fruit, less stodgy cakes and they wouldn't be so pale. Arlene complained that they all had 'bacon and cabbage complexions', and laughed at their attachment to sandwiches; when there was a bread strike she went high and mighty – 'the Lord said that we do not live by bread alone'. She thought that He probably hadn't meant white sliced loaf, and this started off an argument about how much bread they ate in the West Indies.

Each eyed the others' lunches with distaste. The Irish girls wouldn't try anything they weren't used to. Rosemary turned up her nose at Arlene's avocado pear, but also at my salami or curd cheese sandwiches. They used me as a guinea pig, to see if I dropped dead after swallowing a samosa or a slice of mango. However both the Irish and the West Indian women were scathing about the Indians' diet. True, Mrs Patel and her friends seemed to eat only cream crackers at their benches, but they did eat proper lunches in the canteen. The others thought the Indians didn't eat any meat at all and were weak because of it. In fact, Mrs Patel gave me recipes for chicken and lamb curry and complained that her 8-year-old son would only eat fish and chips; but this didn't change their opinion.

The struggle to keep going at such a basic physical level came as a shock to me; I hadn't anticipated what a strain the work would be and resented having to spend so much of my time out of work just recovering. Sleeping and eating became a much more central part of life. The other women

Chapter Seven

Bonus and wages

Every time the light flashed a tray came down the line with another two UMOs for us to assemble. We had no control over the light – how often it flashed was specified in the layout, and the chargehand had set it to the correct speed. We couldn't decide how many UMOs we wanted to do, nor choose to leave one out. The organisation of the line saw to it that we assembled every single one. If you stopped, all the women behind you had to stop as well, less UMOs were made, you lost bonus and so did the others – the tray just stayed at your position until you did your work. Threats of losing bonus and pressure from the other women whose bonus would be lost on your account were usually enough to keep you at it. As carrot and stick the bonus and light ensured continuous production.

How the bonus worked was a mystery – even our pains-taking detective work failed to fathom it completely. We were paid according to 'measured day rate' which meant we had to produce a certain number of UMOs in a certain time to reach the basic rate. Everything we produced on top of that went to the bonus and was paid at the bonus rate. The maximum bonus was £6 a week for 120 points. No one told us how many UMOs we had to assemble for the £6, or what proportion this would be of the total number we did in a week. We didn't have the choice, either individually or as a whole assembly line, to forgo the bonus and work slower. If we worked at top speed with no breakdowns or stoppages all week, we earned more bonus points; but if components ran out or a machine broke down, we earned fewer. No one had a clue how the points were worked out. I asked Eamonn,

Margaret and Carol who could have been in the know as chargehand, training woman and shop steward, but they each came out with a different explanation. After some time it dawned on me that the light was set at top bonus rate – so that we would make up the right number of UMOs, whatever that was, to reach the 120 points so long as there were no hold ups. Any stoppage for whatever reason would reduce the number.

The points remained a mystery until I came to write this book and asked shop steward friends familiar with work study and bonus schemes if they could make head or tail of it. From what they said, it seemed that the bonus must have been calculated on a percentage performance basis. To achieve our basic rate, we would need 100 points or 100 per cent, and the maximum 120 points would have meant 100 per cent performance plus 20 per cent. For 120 points we received an extra £6 on top of our basic rate, so each extra point must have earned us 30p. However, by the time it showed up on our wage slips, the bonus had already been converted into an hourly rate. So the light was set at such a speed that we would automatically do the basic number plus one-fifth to achieve 120 per cent performance.

This revelation made it possible to work out the targets they must have set for the basic rate and the bonus. As we knew how often the light flashed we could also calculate how much we were paid for each UMO on the bonus rate. On the Princess we assembled 60 an hour. This totalled 480 for a day, and 2,400 for the week. Assuming 2,400 represented 120 per cent performance, 100 percent performance would be 2,000 UMOs. This meant we were each paid an extra £6 for doing an extra fifth on top of the 100 per cent, that is, 400 UMOs. Each operator thus received an additional 1½p per UMO on the bonus rate on top of the basic hourly rate, and the whole line of operators an additional 22½p. On the Maxi we assembled 72 an hour, 576 a day and 2,880 in a week. If this was 120 per cent, the basic was 2,400. We did the extra 480 for £6, that is 1¼p per operator per UMO and 18¾p for the whole line.

I've ignored our breaks so these figures aren't completely accurate as we weren't working for the full 8 hours. This would make little difference to the main point: the firm was getting a sixth of the week's output for £6 per operator, and they didn't even have to cajole us into it. No wonder the targets were kept in the dark; given the choice, the women would have preferred to earn £4 less a week, that is, the £6 after tax was deducted, and save themselves the strain and effort of assembling 80 Princess UMOs or 96 Maxi UMOs every day.

We all thought the bonus system a con, but didn't know quite how much of one it was. Not knowing how it worked led to all sorts of wild speculations. Even during the dispute, which was intended to change the bonus system, it was never explained to us. We were under the misapprehension that we needed to produce only a third of normal output to reach the basic rate, and so we assumed that two-thirds of the week's output was being done for £6, working out at a fraction of a penny per UMO. We couldn't imagine that they were sold for much less than £25–30 each; even including the cost of materials, the difference between price and cost must have been large. However we looked at it – and we worked it out several different ways – the firm was paying no more than 29p for the final assembly of a UMO. Our figures were carefully gleaned from wage slips, bonus points, and counting the number of trays. But they must have been the firm's basic data for calculating productivity and profits.

Although we were paid by measured day rate, assemblers were referred to as 'pieceworkers' and this bonus system was the reason. It introduced a piecework element so we were paid by a combination of hourly and piecework rates. For the year February 1977–February 1978, the basic rate was £41.10. This included the previous two years' increases, £6 for 1976 and £2.50 for 1977, but this £8.50 hadn't been formally 'consolidated' into the basic rate. Overtime was paid at time-and-a-third of the old basic of £32.60, so I was told, which made an hourly rate of 81p in comparison with our normal hourly rate of £1.02, so you earned relatively less on a Saturday morning. When the time came for the annual wage round, management wanted to base the increase for 1978 on the official £32.60 basic, not the £41.10. A 10 per cent increase would have amounted to £3.26, making a new basic of £44.36 per week, as compared with £45.21 if it had been based on 10 per cent of £41.10.

The most we could gross in the week was £47.10 including top bonus of 120 points, but this didn't happen very often. For a normal 40-hour week with only a few stoppages, we would gross between £46 and £47, receiving between 112 and 118 bonus points. After deductions for income tax, national insurance and union dues, we took home between £32 and £34 per week. For purposes of comparison let's say our gross average weekly earnings were £46.50 for a 40-hour week, that is £1.16 an hour, though this hourly figure didn't appear on our wage slips. We knew that £46.50 was less than women were paid at some other local factories and also below earnings in Manchester and Sheffield for similar repetitive assembly work. The shortfall was between £5 and £10 a week, due to a difference in the basic rate or in the bonus rate, or a combination of the two. After deductions they would net at least £3-4 more than we did. Our earnings were also approximately £4 below the average for engineering firms covered by private sector collective agreements and well below their hourly rate of £1.23 for 1977.*

So our wages were low for the industry as well as for the area, even if some factories on the Victoria Trading Estate employing a higher proportion of West Indian or particularly Asian women than UMEC did have lower rates of pay. We were close to the national average for our particular section of the engineering industry as a whole, but the higher cost of living in London makes the figure misleading. As we received no London weighting, we were earning relatively less in real terms than women doing similar work in the North, and less still if their absolute earnings were higher than ours and their working week shorter.

I looked in government publications at wage rates and earnings for the relevant period, but it is difficult to make meaningful comparisons. Our weekly average earnings were much the same as the national rates for full-time manual

---

* 'The Pattern of Pay, April 1977: Key Results of the New Earnings Survey', *Department of Employment Gazette*, October 1977.

women workers in our section of the engineering industry; but average hours were lower than ours, between 37 and 38 per week, and the national average hourly rate therefore higher, at £1.18. Looking at it regionally, the average hourly earnings for full-time women workers in the industry in October 1977 were £1.21 in the South East Region, £1.24 in the Greater London sub-region, and average hours worked were 38.1 a week.*

At the time we were getting £46.50, the national average weekly earnings for all full-time women workers over the age of 18 was £51, and women secondary school teachers, for example, were paid £82.30. The gap between men's and women's earnings was large, as one would expect, but I found figures for categories that some of the men at UMEC would fall into. In the non-manual category, electrical engineers were earning £104.80 and electrical technicians £82.30, for a working week of 37.5 hours. In the manual categories, installation and maintenance foremen received £89.90 for a 40-hour week, and foremen in product inspection and repetitive assembling received £82.10. Lower down the scale, men doing the same sort of work as us received about £20 more a week, a difference of about one-third: male repetitive assemblers received a weekly average of £69.30 and packers, bottlers and canners £66.10. This was for 44- and 46-hour weeks, though. Even so, their hourly rates, excluding the effect of overtime, for a basic 40 hours were £1.55 and £1.40.

So someone like Mr Ghandi or the engineer who tormented me were getting more than twice as much as us, for shorter hours, and Arthur Drury and Sean Cooney nearly twice as much. Max would probably have fallen into the £80 bracket as well for inspecting Arlene's filters. The large gap between men's and women's earnings for repetitive assembling nationally doesn't say much for the Equal Pay Act.

UMEC was making even more out of the young workers. Under-eighteens received about £10 a week less than us. The

---

* 'Earnings and Hours of Manual Workers in October 1977', *Department of Employment Gazette*, February 1978.

set-up in the specialist shop meant the women there received the same bonus as us, but made up considerably more UMOs on their individual targets. They were far less militant than women on the line – maybe their individual bonus encouraged them to believe that if they worked harder they would earn more.

After the annual pay round in February, our wages went up, but the differential between UMEC and the firms we compared it with was maintained. There was a lot of agitation about the increase; we demanded consolidation of the previous two years' increases into the basic wage, and a 30 per cent increase on the consolidated rate. An extra 10 bonus highest paid food factory in Victoria Trading Estate. After much to-ing and fro-ing, consolidation was granted, and a 10 per cent increased on the consolidated rate. An extra 10 bonus points, bringing it up to 130, and 50p we won in the dispute, raised the bonus to a new maximum of £7. In addition, the new self-financing productivity scheme meant that everyone in the factory, including management, got an extra 6 per cent, paid monthly so long as there had been no industrial dispute or stoppage. For us, this amounted to £12 a month – however, we considered it one more attempt at divide and rule because it made disputes unpopular with workers not directly involved.

After these various increases, we could now gross about £55 in a 'good' week with top bonus and no stoppages, taking home around £38. But from April there was an additional deduction when contributions to a pension scheme became compulsory. We had the choice of joining UMEC's private scheme or the state scheme, but the advantages of either were not clearly presented. Most women thought UMEC got enough out of us anyway, and were reluctant to give them more 'to invest and make even more profits out of us'. However, the private scheme included an arrangement for burial expenses, which won Rosemary over. If she died here at least they'd pay for her body to be sent home to Ireland.

Rumour had it that UMEC was attempting to break down the division between manual and non-manual workers. As the division seemed well and truly entrenched on the shop-floor, I wondered what on earth this meant. It turned out to be the granting of 'staff' status to manual workers. After several years' service sick pay and holiday entitlements became more like those of the engineers, and even before April 1978, they were allowed to join UMEC's pension scheme. The *Times Business News* used to crow about this sort of policy as a way of counterbalancing the effect of the Labour government's wages policy. By receiving increased 'fringe benefits' manual workers could be shown to do as well out of pay policy and percentage wage increases as non-manual workers through this addition to their 'social wage'. However, it didn't take a mathematician to calculate that a 10 per cent increase for an engineer on £6,000 or £8,000 a year was more than for a skilled man on £70 a week even after adding on the sick pay and holiday benefits.

From the shopfloor this policy didn't look like kindness, nor did it break down any divisions. It looked more like an attempt to give the men some perks that might make it worth their while to stay at UMEC. They probably wanted to reduce labour turnover amongst the assemblers as well. Many women stayed between one and two years. After two years they were less inclined to leave because of the sick pay and extra couple of days' holiday. Rosemary wanted a better-paying job, but she reckoned it was worth staying to hang on to these perks. It took about ten years to get a whole two weeks' sick pay and extra holiday. The 'staff' system separated the women into different groups, making more divisions rather than reducing them. It was often trotted out along with the bonus and extra 2p for the more 'responsible' jobs on the line, as a reason to work harder, stay longer and prove what a good employer we had. However, it was a big decision to take time off when you were ill if you hadn't yet been there for two years – you wouldn't get National Insurance sickness benefit for the first three days. Being ill could cost you a lot of money.

The interest and emotion aroused by a few pennies and pounds may seem odd to someone who has never worked on the shopfloor. When I had a secure monthly salary large enough to live on, arriving regularly in the bank, I couldn't understand all the excitement. Friends of mine compared wages, discussed what they could and couldn't afford to buy and talked incessantly about prices. My attitude changed completely as a result of being in the same situation. The minutiae of wage settlements, bonus rates, and overtime pay were not trivial issues in the least. For one thing, there was so little money that you had to make sure you received every penny you were entitled to, because it really did count. For another, you couldn't trust that the correct amount would automatically be paid. Our wage slips were different every week: sometimes the productivity bonus wasn't paid, with no explanation given. Sometimes the bonus was much too low on our estimation of the pace of work the previous week – then we accused the chargehands of fiddling the sheets showing how many UMOs had been assembled each day. Sometimes there were delays in sorting out tax, holiday and sick pay.

Every Thursday we scrutinised the wage slips to make sure we hadn't been diddled; invariably a few people would be missing something. For a three-week stretch we received no bonus payments because the computer punch card operators were on strike and the bonus points couldn't be incorporated into the payroll. During the month of the foremen's strike, the productivity scheme bonus wasn't paid, and we also lost our bonus for the time we had to stop working while they were on their work to rule. When the pension scheme started there were a lot of anomalies to be sorted out. After a run of irregular wages for several weeks, we voted unanimously at a union meeting to down tools 'next time management mucks around with the wages'. We were fed up, even though it was partly due to other sections of the work force and not management. But we never knew what was happening, and had to badger the supervisors to get an explanation.

The computer strike meant we didn't know where we stood money-wise. One week they gave us a sum for the bonus based on the previous week's pay slip, and promised to rectify any anomalies when the strike was over. Many women expected they'd be docked money in future weeks because of this, and complained about having to go short through no fault of their own. They had done their work and fulfilled their side of the contract – the firm should do the same, and pay up at the right time. Irregularities in the pay slips caused a lot of aggravation, and several women asked me if I was thinking of leaving because there had been so much mucking around with the wages during the time I'd been there. With such a small wage, weekly budgeting, and hire purchase instalments to repay weekly, it was vital to know where you stood, and be able to rely on a steady income – otherwise you were put out completely and had nothing to fall back on.

Everyone was very quick at mental arithmetic when it came to working out the new percentage increases, and the different elements that went into making up the total wage. This was from weekly practice at examining wage slips and working out if they'd been credited with the correct amount, and that deductions for tax and insurance were in order. I looked forward to my pay packet – somehow the money seemed more when you got it in your hand and you felt as if you'd really earned it. The extra or missing pennies represented directly that we'd been very hard pushed or that a hold up had affected the bonus. The payment for hours worked, with a quarter-of-an-hour lopped off if you were three minutes late in the morning, or if you had taken time off for going to the doctor or dentist, made you very aware of selling your labour, and that the firm had the rights over your 40 hours at work. Not being allowed to read during a hold up even made some sort of sense when you realised they were paying you for the time you did nothing. Money was what you were there for, and it was up to you to decide if you could afford a couple of hours off for a medical appointment. They even docked you if you had to make an urgent phone call. In comparison, a monthly salary in the bank seemed like a grant rather than payment for labour, and the relation between time and money very obscure.

Our take-home pay was too low for a single person to live on. It was married women's wages, based on the assumption that there was a higher male income for you to fall back on. Most of the married women depended on their husband's wage for basic living – their own going towards clothes, holidays and savings. But most single women had to take a second job just to make ends meet. Rosemary and Nora had their regular cleaning jobs, and Margaret worked as a barmaid. Ann and Eileen did all the overtime they could. I was the only one on our line who never did overtime. For single mothers it was even harder. Grace boosted her wages a bit through commission on the mail order catalogue she brought in – she couldn't take another job because of Yvonne. Many of the others ordered clothes through her, and paid her back in weekly instalments. The garments arrived at her house by post and she brought them into work. Her whole weekend seemed to be taken up with filling in order forms and repacking clothes that didn't fit. At first, I wasn't interested in the catalogues and thought them a waste of money because the clothes cost more than in the shops. Jeans cost £16 from the catalogue but you could easily get them for £12 in local shops and all the T-shirts and cotton blouses were over £5. But you simply couldn't afford to buy an item of clothing in one go out of your wages, because you wouldn't have enough money for the rest of the week. So you had to pay more in the long run because you couldn't afford to fork out a smaller amount in one go. People who earned more could buy things cheaper without getting into debt, or taking on interest repayments.

There was more to the catalogues than staggered payments. After work you had so little time and so many chores to cram into the weekend, that there wasn't time to browse round the shops looking for clothes. Many women found the catalogues a convenient time-saving method of shopping. Choosing a dress or skirt gave you something to fantasise about while you were working. You could take days to choose which one you wanted and get everyone else's advice. Thinking about the new clothes took your mind off the work, and you could look forward to the clothes arriving.

The money completely determined how you shopped. Before working at UMEC, when things were reduced in the supermarket I used to buy up a whole load, or go to Boots and buy up all the toiletries I'd need for the next three months. This was impossible on a UMEC wage. I started leaving until the following week what I could manage without, even when it was reduced, because buying it would leave me short of something I really needed. By Tuesday many of the single girls were borrowing money. Josey borrowed from her mum every week. Veronica from the sweet factory ate only cheese rolls after Tuesday because she wouldn't borrow any money from the rest of us. Eileen's diet of Crunchie bars and a bowl of soup at night was also because she had no money.

The low level of wages meant that considering a work to rule or strike was a very serious step. We were living from week to week and day to day. When wages were cut, the married women were better off because they could fall back on their husbands, but single women just couldn't afford to lose pay. It seemed a terrible irony that those who were worst off found it hardest to take any action to improve their conditions. The Leyland toolroom men were better off than us and could put a bit aside; it would be easier for them to forgo a week's pay to improve their earnings in the long run. When we received no pay during the suspension, many of the young single girls had to leave and get another job even though they supported the action – they just couldn't manage without a regular weekly income.

Chapter Eight
The union and the dispute

The union

There was a closed shop in the factory. At the interview they told you union membership was required and asked if you minded. Arthur Drury told me that pay and work conditions had been worked out with the union's agreement.

There were about 600 women 'pieceworkers' in the Industrial Workers and Technicians Union (IWTU), those of us in the main assembly, Assembly 2, the valve shop and the sprocket shop. The other manual workers from the machine shop and the few skilled men were in a different union but this had a much smaller membership than ours as did the other trade unions representing supervisors, progress chasers, lorry drivers and other grades. The chargehands were in the same union as us, but belonged to a different branch.

Union dues were deducted weekly from our wages, and the main negotiating body for the manual workers was the Works Committee. Each shop had its own steward, and the Works Committee was elected from the stewards; one full-time convenor headed the Works Committee.

The women on the line were pretty negative about the union's activities in the factory. They said they were never told what was going on, and only learnt about decisions after they affected the wage packet. They were kept in the dark, their views weren't properly represented, and the dues of 30p a week were too high for the service they got. The union officials were seen more or less as part of the firm's authority structure along with management, and equally remote. Between them they made the decisions, but the negotiations were shrouded in mystery and aroused rumour and mistrust. The IWTU was accused of being a 'management union', allowing the firm to impose whatever conditions it liked. Some women thought the union was the major obstacle to any improvements. They said the Works Committee had been run by the same small gang for years and years, and felt that the convenor's retirement was long overdue. The convenor was a woman IWTU steward, Maisie Dibbs. She was English, over seventy and said to have been convenor for thirty years. She sold free-range eggs from a hut at her disposal on the premises, and ran a raffle that no one had ever been known to win, or so the joke went. Rumour had it that she was brought to work in a company car. Whatever the truth behind the rumours, the general feeling was that Maisie Dibbs and the rest of the Works Committee had been 'bought off' in small ways, and were 'for the firm'. They couldn't be relied on to stick up for the women's point of view. Many of the older stewards were dismissed as Maisie Dibbs's 'cronies'; they had also held their posts for decades, and echoed her opinions. However, Mrs Dibbs was credited with fighting for individual cases of hardship when people hadn't received the right holiday or sick pay. But on major issues they said she took the firm's side at worst, and at best acted only as an intermediary between us and the firm.

It was quite surprising then that the women took any action or attended union meetings, but the distrust was confined to the officials. Most of the women were greatly in favour of the union and often said that they, the women on the line, were the union. If they didn't stand up for themselves, no one else would; they were the real union, not Maisie Dibbs and her gang. They trusted Carol, the shop steward they had elected the year before to replace one of Mrs Dibbs's cronies, and thought it would be much better if all the stewards were like her.

The women chose Carol because she stood up for them and wasn't frightened of anyone. She was twenty-one, came from a left-wing background, and had a Young Socialist tattoo on her arm. She was English, born of Irish parents, and quite different from the other women. She had a tough Cockney manner and would never back down in an argument or admit she was in the wrong. She always wore old jeans, which the women would have criticised in anyone else, and rode a motorbike. Her sister had also worked at UMEC and been militant. Carol said she had been eased out, and was finding it difficult to get another job locally. Carol was quite capable of shouting at Arthur Drury till she was red in the face, and wouldn't be cowed by any of the men.

We held union meetings 'at the back of the line' between 12.30 and 12.45 (in our own time) but there were no branch meetings outside the factory. When something cropped up, Carol sent a notice in a tray up the lines announcing a lunch-time meeting. Not many weeks went by without one, and sometimes there were several. Attendance had risen greatly since Carol took over. Her job at the top of the middle line made her visible to all, and there was great interest if she talked to the supervisors, or was called out to a meeting. As soon as she came back, everyone wanted to know what was happening. She wanted to increase the number of stewards, and eventually succeeded in getting each line to elect its own, so there would be one steward for every fifteen women instead of just one for the whole shop. Then issues could be taken up more quickly, and complaints about incorrect pay slips dealt with immediately.

Despite grumbling about the union, even the more vociferous women were reluctant to take up a steward's post. Some of them thought you would stick your neck out, and then be let down by everyone else; they didn't really trust the others to back them if it came to the crunch. Rosemary and a couple of other young Irish women became stewards in the end – they had no previous experience, and wouldn't dare chair meetings. Rosemary was good at reporting back, and wrote down long notes for Nora and Mary.

The picture I got of the Works Committee was confusing. It seemed odd that there should be a woman convenor on a largely male shop stewards' committee, and also odd that the representatives of the semi-skilled workers in the IWTU held higher posts than the more skilled men. I never got a clear idea of what the Works Committee did – whether, for example, it could negotiate over line speed and work conditions as well as pay. But lack of information was an indictment in itself.

We were in the dark about official union procedure, and didn't know whether or not we were covered by national agreements between the Confederation of Shipbuilding and Engineering Unions and the Engineering Employers' Federation. Our basic pay rates and holiday allowances were below the nationally agreed levels, so I assumed everything was locally negotiated.

On the other hand, it was also odd that the women had let the Works Committee continue year after year if they thought it so bad. They blamed this on each other, 'you know what the girls here are like. . . '. There had been a big defeat about fifteen years before when they lost a strike, and they said Mrs Dibbs had been in control ever since. I think the high proportion of 'green labour' must have made a difference, isolating the women who knew the score from those not used to factory work or unions. Nevertheless, most of the new Irish women were pro-union although many boyfriends and husbands worked 'on the lump' in the building industry.

The dispute starts

It began over a small issue, then blew up. Frustration over the previous few years' small increases had been building up and turned into the biggest dispute seen for twenty years.

A union meeting was called at the back of the line to discuss the firm's proposed productivity deal. We had been offered a 3 per cent increase for two months which would have worked out at about 50p a week after tax. Several explanations of the offer had been given: first it was a 'gift', then it was due to savings on wastage, materials and heating. It was rejected by all the women; they were insulted by the offer of a few pennies and indignant that the firm should expect them to be grateful. Instead, a demand was put in to double the bonus rate from £5 a week to £10, and management was given one week's notice to arrange it; otherwise all the lines would start a go slow. I didn't understand the £5 and £10 because the top bonus was £6, but never mind. The women thought the bonus was rubbish in any case, and that it was more important to go for an increase in the basic rate. But the annual wage round wasn't due till February, and it was only October. They thought that raising the bonus was different from a wage increase, and would fall outside of the pay policy then in force. We didn't know that threatening a go slow wasn't 'agreed procedure' and no one bothered to inform us. Later we learnt that you had to give 48 hours' notice of going off piecework and onto the measured day rate before our union would recognise you to be acting according to procedure.

The main assembly goes slow

The dispute developed day to day over the next few weeks. By the following Friday no news had come from management about the bonus demand. As that was the deadline, the six lines in the main assembly started a go slow from 9 in the morning. Nobody knew what to do, so we just did half the work, and instructed the women feeding the light to miss out every other tray. In the afternoon, Mrs Dibbs and some of the Works Committee called us to a meeting at the back of the line. This was the first time I'd met her, but I recognised her as the woman who sold eggs, and Rosemary and I called her the 'egg woman' after that. They looked like the Mafia I'd been told about. She was a white-haired, rather large lady wearing carpet slippers. Her main henchman was tubby and bald, with an impressive curly moustache. He wore a boiler suit. They reprimanded us for the go slow and urged us to return to 'normal working'; nothing could happen until we went 'through procedure' – but they didn't explain what the procedure was. In any case, they said, we wouldn't get anything until February.

They took the vote to return to work four times. Each time it was unanimously rejected. First, we all voted not to return to 'normal', then Mrs Dibbs said we would have to be working normally for the Works Committee to negotiate on our behalf. She put the next motion to the vote: 'Do you want the Works Committee to negotiate for you?' No one was taken in by this, and Carol suggested an overtime ban, which was adopted. This retaking of the vote was to become a feature of the following weeks, and we became thoroughly fed up with it. We continued going slow the following week. Every day the Works Committee called us to several meetings. At one, Mrs Dibbs said they were suggesting to both workers and management that our pay should be increased by 1p an hour; this was rejected as laughable. At each meeting they told us to return to normal work, on the grounds that they couldn't do anything for us while we were working 'abnormally'.

The atmosphere on the shopfloor was very good. We read at the same time as we worked, and went to the loo when we liked. There was time to chat and to talk to women on the next line whom we didn't know very well. We got up from our chairs whenever we felt like it. It was almost as if we'd taken over the place – we ignored the normal discipline of the line and Arthur Drury could do nothing about it. We took charge of the stop-clock ourselves because we suspected they might speed up the actual line. Everyone commented on how few rejects there were, and said this was the right pace for working. There was time to do the job properly and we weren't nearly so tired by the end of the afternoon. Each time a meeting was called, we got up from our benches and left the UMOs half done. Chargehands and supervisors looked on helplessly.

The Works Committee seemed to think we'd get so fed up with meetings that we'd give in. One of Mrs Dibbs's cronies tried to confuse us at one meeting by reporting that management was ready to negotiate the productivity deal with us – but she was told in no uncertain terms that we were concerned about the bonus, not a productivity deal. Then she said management had agreed to employ someone permanently on the shopfloor to iron out grievances about layouts, rejects and details of individual jobs. We said this wasn't the issue either. Finally, she reported that management was sorry they'd ever mentioned the 3 per cent bonus and was now withdrawing it; but half an hour later she called another meeting to tell us management was giving us the 3 per cent as a gift.

Mrs Dibbs herself also emphasised that management was 'aware of the problems of you pieceworkers', 'they know how difficult it is for you girls to pay the rent', and so on. This infuriated the women more than anything else that week: 'why don't they come and pay our rent when we are off sick if they are so concerned?' One young Asian woman shouted at Mrs Dibbs that what we spent our money on was nothing to do with management; we didn't want to be paid for the rent and food, but wanted the rate for the job and a decent wage. Everyone cheered and there was much indignation at management pretending to be concerned about hardship just as it suited them, as well as disgust at Mrs Dibbs speaking on management's behalf, and trying to win our sympathies by bringing up red herrings like the rent. Whenever Mrs Dibbs insisted that it was a pay rise we were demanding she was howled down; Carol and the others shouted that we wanted an increase in the bonus payment and this was different. Everyone was discussing what the wages were in other local firms, and agreed that our pay was £20 less than in the American-owned food factory where their friends cleared £50 a week and could always do overtime.

In the middle of this first week of the go slow, management sent letters to each of us informing us that our pay would be cut by half. Rosemary collected them up and handed them back to Arthur Drury – that was our way of saying that we didn't accept what they said. Some women suggested a mass meeting so all the pieceworkers would be able to discuss the situation, but older women warned that there hadn't been a mass meeting for eighteen years, and thought Mrs Dibbs would permit one only over her dead body. She told us that she had been onto the 'outside union' (i.e. the IWTU regional offices), to make management drop its threat of half-pay, and again suggested returning to normal work. This was interpreted as her pretending to be on our side, and we demanded a mass meeting. We gathered outside in the 'yard' near the canteen and were joined by women from the sprocket shop, valve shop and from Assembly 2 for the meeting. To Mrs Dibbs's dismay, they voted overwhelmingly to join us in the go slow – there was only a brief discussion as they were so sure they wanted to join us. We were confused as to whether the firm really could cut our pay by half, but Carol thought that if we were clocking in, were present and working for

40 hours, they had to go on paying us, even if we were supposed to produce 50 per cent or 33 per cent of our normal output to reach our basic pay. This issue was the root of our misunderstanding of how the bonus system worked – but Mrs Dibbs didn't enlighten us.

One day I was moved to the newly opened Continental line where the go slow was more difficult to enforce. There was no light, and Kurt put the trays out on the line at irregular intervals as the jobs hadn't yet been timed. Flocks of engineers were standing about. It was all a bit intimidating. Anna and Bridie were electrical checking behind me; most of the time they were deep in calculations about the number of UMOs assembled each hour, day, week, month and year, and how we were diddled by the bonus. They wanted to get back copies of the company reports that were distributed to the women every year, so as to have more exact information.

On Friday, a week after we began the go slow, we received notices that we would be suspended unless we returned to normal work by Monday. Rosemary handed these back too. Everyone said we must stick it out now, because the firm must be losing work and getting rattled. The tables were turned at the daily Works Committee vote about returning to work – we passed a unanimous vote of no confidence in them. On the way home, Alice and I met a woman from the sprocket shop walking up the High Street whom neither of us knew. But she knew we were from the Main Assembly and encouraged us to stick it out. 'The whole place will be "out" on Monday if any one of you is suspended.' She hated Mrs Dibbs and said it was vital to get rid of the Works Committee, and stop blacklegs working.

Suspension – the other manual workers join us

In fact we weren't suspended until the Wednesday. When we arrived we found our clock cards had been removed and the lines weren't running, so we couldn't work. We voted to sit in. On hearing the news, workers in the valve shop, press shop, and, more important, the machine shop, downed tools in support of us but continued to clock in. Assembly 2 carried on with their go slow. Mrs Dibbs came to make a last appeal: the outside union would come to negotiate for us during the next two to three weeks, but we would have to return to work in the meantime. She was talking as if we had chosen to stop work rather than having been suspended. We rejected the offer but asked for another mass meeting – our decision now affected the many other workers who had stopped work on our behalf and they would suffer if we rejected the offer. So we wanted them to decide whether or not we should give in.

We marched to the yard in one group, and all the men in the machine shop cheered and clapped as we went by. At least 600 people attended this mass meeting, standing on rickety tables and clinging to rusty old skips to see and hear what was happening. The crowd looked very impressive and there was a great feeling of determination and optimism. The chair was taken by a steward Mrs Dibbs thought would be more popular than herself. All the women from the main assembly were told to stand at the back as we weren't to vote, and the rest were in the front. The majority were women, but there was a handful of West Indian and Asian men from the stores and machine shop. Two black men next to me said the Works Committee deserved to be shot, and that we must stay out now; the women had everyone else's support at present, but couldn't be sure of it in two weeks' time, especially if we went back to work in between.

The chairman twisted the information in an effort to persuade everyone back to work, and Carol had to take over the megaphone to put him straight. He said to those workers who hadn't been suspended, 'if you agree, the girls in dispute will go back for two weeks' – implying that was what we wanted them to do, rather than the opposite. He fudged the issue of when exactly the outside union would come in – now, in three weeks, or when they had time. The others voted 'to stay put until a concrete offer' was made to us, but the vote had to be retaken several times before the chairman would accept it, even though it was unanimous. Several men stood up and warned that the women shouldn't accept any vague promises of negotiations.

Everyone was bubbling over with excitement for the

rest of the day. Carol went round telling the women how important it was that we sat in all day and didn't go home so as to show management that we were united and determined to see it through. Doreen brought in Monopoly and Snakes and Ladders the next day, and we played games. Other women had cards and we swapped round all our games. Josey brought her radio so we could have some music, and everyone handed round their magazines. We sat in groups up and down the shop, chatting and knitting. Everyone was very friendly and the atmosphere was quite jolly. Some of us decided to go and look round the parts of the factory we'd never seen, and we visited the sprocket shop. The women seemed very militant there, and we had a sing-song of Irish rebel songs. In the valve room the women showed us how they assembled our valves, and we made friends with the workers in the machine shop next door. This started a trend – soon workers from the other shops started wandering all over the place as well and came to visit us in the main assembly. We showed them what work we did. Everyone agreed how silly it was we'd never met before, and that it was the firm that had kept us apart.

I'll interrupt this account of the dispute, to report on the conversation we had with one of the women who worked in the machine shop.

Woman in the machine shop

I went into the machine shop with Anna and Bridie the second day we were suspended. A circle of men and women were sitting round; they'd downed tools the day before. All the machine shop workers had stopped work except one, and he'd been persuaded during the course of the day.

We talked for a long time to one woman. I don't know her name. She was about the same age as Anna, in her fifties, and had a slight Polish accent. She was slim and blonde with a pinched face, looked rather drawn, and was neatly dressed in skirt, jumper and overalls. She told us about the work in there; there were about twenty-five machines, mostly making washers and small metal bits for our UMOs, from large coils of metal weighing up to 80lbs. The metal was valuable and the supervisor had to weigh the scrap when they had finished to make sure the workers hadn't pinched any. It was Dickensian in there. The machines looked ancient and were covered in rust and oil; there was a cold hard cement floor and no seats to sit on during work. She said they had no proper place to hang their coats or put their food, only old oil drums – if you put your things on them they got oily.

This woman showed us how the machines worked. She had to fix a coil of metal onto the machine. The number of washers it made was pre-set, and she collected them in a tray on the other side of the machine. To reach full bonus she had to make 7,500 washers an hour, but the machine was set at 7,200 so she could never reach it. The coils had to be changed every twenty minutes, and she lost bonus while she fixed on the new one. She had to watch the machine all the time, and couldn't go to the loo unless she worked with someone else and took turns. There wasn't equal pay because labourers lifted the heaviest coils for the women, but she didn't mind.

The machines were switched on all day except during lunchtime and the 9.50–10 a.m. tea-break, but, unlike the main assembly, they had no informal breaks. The machine noise was deafening, and they could only talk to each other in sign language. They'd been given earmuffs as protection, but couldn't wear them – they were all a standard size and gave most people a terrible headache. She said she heard the noise of the machines all night, like a permanent deafening thud in her ears. They didn't wear the protective gloves as these got in the way when fiddling with the machine, although they ought to have because of the oil. Several of them had dermatitis.

We asked how come she was so clean if it was such filthy work, and she said she wore a clean jumper every day and got through two cardigans and two skirts a week. She emphasised what terrible work it was, standing on your feet all day in the noise and dirt, but she thought that many of the women in assembly looked down on the machine shop workers. 'They shouldn't just because they do cleaner work, and anyway they need the components we make in here.'

She said she could stick at the job only 'because they are such a wonderful crowd in here'. Everyone pulled together, and looked after each other – otherwise she would have left long ago. She hadn't a bad word to say against any of them, and she thought that was the reason they all stayed. One of the Indian labourers had been a bit remote to begin with but now he mucked in, too, and the labourers came round regularly to see that the women were all right and had enough coils.

She told us that sometimes management brought visitors round. These were mainly students who stood ignoring her, not lifting a finger while she was trying to lift a heavy coil; she often thought of dropping it on their feet. It would look like an accident, but she thought better of it, and didn't let herself be tempted to be silly.

She demonstrated the movements she had to make all day for us, and explained it all very clearly. She made a deep impression on all of us, as she looked so worn and tired and yet had so much spirit. Anna and Bridie thought they wouldn't be able to stand the work for more than two minutes. They thought it dreadful that although we worked only next door, we hadn't known what conditions were like in the machine shop. After that we often walked through there on our way to the canteen, and you really had to block your ears when the machines were on. I couldn't get the Polish woman out of my mind for several days. She spoke to us in such a straightforward way, not trying to elicit pity or emotion, but was proud and interested to show us how the work was done. She had downed tools automatically on our behalf when we were suspended, but wouldn't get anything out of it herself. We doubted whether the women in assembly would do the same for the machine shop. The worse the work conditions, it seemed, the greater the solidarity and the more spontaneous the workers' response.

Returning to the dispute, when our pay packets arrived for the week covering the go slow, we were pleased to find we were only about £3 down on our normal wages. We had lost only the bonus money. This was encouraging, because it 'proved' to us that we normally did half the work in the week for under £3 clear, a mistaken view as I've already explained. During the first few days of suspension there would be a vote every few hours about reviewing the decision to stay out; by the end of the week we refused to go to any more meetings until an offer was made. The women were convinced that the Works Committee was trying to divide us, and create cracks by getting one or two women to admit they would rather be working. Mrs Dibbs was rumoured to have called the police when some women picketed the swing-shift who were still working in the evenings.

After a week of suspension, some women were beginning to get a little bored, and Carol had to jolly them along. She was very cross with women who started drifting off in the afternoon. There was a strong feeling that something would have to break soon, either an offer or a proper lockout. But the chargehands had been covering up all the machines as if laying down for a siege. Most of us carried on chatting and reading; I learnt some new stitches from an Irish girl who was knitting a very intricate Arran sweater. A lot of arithmetic was being done all the time, calculating profits, numbers of UMOs and how much the firm would be losing. We had time to do it properly now.

'Outside' union officials came for a meeting with us during the second week of suspension. We spent the morning formulating questions to put to them. Mrs Dibbs was dressed up for the meeting, with lipstick and shoes, and it was held in the canteen with a microphone. The official from the other manual workers' union implied that we should stick it out if we really wanted to achieve anything, and was warmly applauded, but our representative from the IWTU didn't say anything new and seemed very nervous. They reported that management had now offered £1.25 a week as fall-back rate, pending a productivity scheme, but that they were not prepared to discuss the bonus at all. This fall-back rate would mean a guaranteed £1.25 a week if, for any reason, we couldn't make our bonus. So the choice was to accept this £1.25 or carry on demanding the £5 which they said was already 'in procedure', to be negotiated at some unspecified future date. We called for another mass meeting of all piece-workers to decide about the £1.25 as we felt it ought to be decided by all those who were now involved.

The mass meeting took place in the canteen that afternoon, and everyone could sit down for a change. All 600 were there, and the meeting lasted a couple of hours. There was a terrific feeling and the momentum reached its highest point then. The fall-back rate offer was quickly rejected by about 550 votes to 10, and we voted to 'stay as we are until management makes a sensible offer'. Everyone was solid despite attempts by the Works Committee to call for seconders after the vote had been taken. A committee of pieceworkers was set up, like a strike committee, to deal with hardship cases, organise the day and negotiate on our behalf, as there were no pieceworkers on the Works Committee. A heated discussion ensued about how the swing-shift could be stopped from working. Our antagonism towards them had increased because management used them to blackleg while we were suspended and they had ignored our appeals to stop working. Without them the factory would have ground to a standstill. The Works Committee assured the meeting that they would instruct management to tell the evening workers not to report for work. We doubted later that this had ever been carried out. Carol said that most of the swing-shift were single mothers, desperate for the work and money, and only able to work at night, so we should really have found a better way of sorting out our differences with them.

There were no more developments the rest of that week, but the mass meeting had boosted morale and brought us all together again. Everyone was enthusiastic about sitting it out. Money was getting tight, though, and some of the young single girls had to start looking for part-time jobs. Josey and her friend had to move out of their bedsit and back to Mum because they couldn't pay the rent and everyone was behind on their HP payments and telly money.

Divided and defeated

The final dénouement began on the Friday, three weeks after we started the go slow. The Works Committee proposed to negotiate a £5 increase for everyone at UMEC, not just the pieceworkers, again pending a productivity scheme. They would suggest this to management, and whatever offer management made would be put to a meeting of all workers in the factory. We would have to abide by the majority decision to accept or not. It took about an hour for the implications of this to sink in, and then people were furious. It would mean an increase for employees of all UMEC's factories, including management, so ditching our claim and our attempt to decrease differentials between the lowest paid and the rest. The shop stewards' committee rejected the proposal, so at this stage it turned out to be a false alarm.

The next week was the fourth since the dispute began and morale went up and down in big swings during the days. Again we felt sure that something had to happen soon. The day seemed very long, and some women skived off in the afternoon or didn't come in at all, which made the others very ratty. They thought the absentees wouldn't refuse the increase when it came, so they ought to stick it out with the rest of us, not just leave it to others to fight their battle. There was even suspicion at our own pieceworkers' committee when it had no news to report – people felt they were being kept in the dark, and Joyce brought up the whole question of democratic representation again.

One lunchtime, management offered us 50p a week, as an extra 10 per cent on the bonus. Naturally this was rejected, but it was welcomed as being the first sign that they were at last prepared to make offers on the bonus, which had been 'out of the question' up to now. A mass meeting was called for 4 p.m. that day, when most of us had gone home: an offer of £2.20 for all workers and 50p extra for the piece-work workers was to be put to the vote.

When it emerged the next morning that this was a repeat of Friday's ploy of offering something to all workers, it was quickly dismissed as another trick to defeat us in whatever way they could. One woman stressed that it would cost the firm much more to give everyone this extra money than to settle our claim. The supervisors were definitely up to something, getting the benches ready and putting out screws and nuts, and the factory buzzed with rumours. All the high-ups were acting as if they knew we would be back at work by the end of the week, but we didn't know why.

On the Wednesday morning, two weeks after we'd been suspended, a mass meeting was called for all manual workers. This included the chargehands, maintenance men, quality control, lorry drivers and men from the stores. Representatives of management were lurking at the back, apparently invited by the Works Committee to watch the proceedings. This was to be the final showdown. All the women sat down, determined not to be railroaded, and all the 'white coats' stood around in small groups looking rather embarrassed. The Works Committee controlled the microphone and wouldn't permit any discussion. They put an offer to the whole meeting and called for the vote immediately. The offer was £3 for everyone, plus an extra 50p for the pieceworkers for a two-month period pending 'investigation of anomalies'.

The women decided not to take part in this vote, as the tactics were clear, but the chairman asked those in favour of acceptance to move to the right and vice versa. As we were sitting across the whole room, the chairman said he would count anyone sitting down as being 'for' the proposal. So we had to stand up, but by then the vote was almost over. The vote was split fairly evenly even taking into account the men's votes, but the tellers didn't bother to count, they just announced that the majority was 'for'. This was interpreted by the Works Committee as meaning we should now return to work.

We were in disarray, angry, frustrated, and feeling totally manipulated. Some women saw it as confirmation that we should never have tried to take on the firm in the first place, as they were so much stronger, and we were bound to lose. Carol and a couple of the other stewards resigned (temporarily) because of the way the meeting had been railroaded. Now there was no one to speak for us, no leadership, and nobody knew what to do. It wasn't up to us to decide to return to work, we said: the firm had prevented us from working by removing our clock cards. They would have to ask us back. Throughout the dispute, both union and management had turned this into its opposite, making out it was us who had refused to work, till we almost believed it ourselves. The meeting had been a classic and successful divide and rule – bringing in people who weren't involved and offering them something for nothing which they would naturally accept, and then using this against us. No one was really surprised – they expected as much from the Works Committee.

Meanwhile our clock cards had been replaced, and the few women who hadn't sat in drifted back into the main assembly in ones and twos. By the end of the afternoon they were able to start up one assembly line. Once this happened, morale plummeted amongst the rest of us because we had been split. If some women had gone back, they said, others would gradually follow – so we'd lost. As we were excluded from our shops, we sat in the canteen all day, and, making a last-ditch stand, demanded back-pay for the time we had been suspended. We discussed what on earth to do, and there was much hostility towards those who had returned to work. At one point, the works manager came in, and had the tea and coffee machines disconnected and switched off the lights, to make it as uncomfortable as possible for us.

The following morning, Thursday, about 300 of us turned up again in the canteen and conducted a continuous meeting for several hours. There was growing hysteria about people returning to work and little idea how to prevent it. The issue turned into how best to secure the back-pay, as even the outside union official had conceded that the firm had been wrong to suspend us. Many suggestions were made: picketing the factory, storming the works manager's office, an all-out strike, but none was seriously taken up. Finally, a vote was taken to return to work, but only on the understanding that management met our stewards at 2 p.m. that afternoon about the back pay. The majority of women from the main assembly voted against this proposal but there was a general feeling that it would be more dignified to decide to give up the sit in ourselves, than to dribble back slowly, and let them see who the real militants were.

Return to work

Late in the morning we trudged back to the main assembly, very dejected. They were ready for us, all the components were laid out, and the supervisors told us where to sit and to start working. We felt a bit sheepish, and didn't speak to any of the women who had returned the day before. Eamonn seemed keen to 'get rolling' again, and Arthur Drury treated us like naughty children, clearly pleased to assert his authority again.

The tyranny of the line took over straight away, and it was as if there had never been a break – except we got tired very quickly because we weren't used to the speed. I 'forgot' to put washers under my screws and didn't screw them down tight enough, until Eamonn caught me. Even though we'd said we wouldn't worry about keeping up with the line while we were going slow, you just had to try or else loads of trays piled up in front of you and you would have to do them sooner or later.

There was uproar the next morning when we learnt that management had refused to see our stewards about the back-pay – we'd gone back on false promises. Over the next weeks there were countless meetings about the back-pay; ours was never paid, but the other union gave strike pay for the relevant period to its members in the machine shop because their action had been made official. Many women in the main assembly wanted to leave the IWTU and join the other union instead, but this was against the Bridlington Agreement and impossible.

We also learnt that British Leyland had had to stop six assembly lines because of shortages of UMOs. We felt sick that we had had management in the palm of our hands with their main customers badly affected, but had let them get away with it. On the other hand, it was rumoured that the UMEC factory in Scotland, where our transistors were made, had also been in dispute, and that their dispute and ours had finished on exactly the same day. This indicated that the entire showdown had been orchestrated from above, and we even wondered whether the firm had in fact welcomed our dispute and the chance to suspend us; we wouldn't have been able to work without transistors in any event, but they would have had to pay our basic wages.

The following week we attempted to get better stewards onto the Works Committee. Each line elected its own steward – women who had spoken up over the past weeks, like Rosemary, Bridie and the young Asian woman. There had been several votes of no confidence in the Works Committee, and

Mrs Dibbs and her cronies stressed that we could throw them all out in the annual elections. But when the new stewards went along to elect members for the Works Committee, they found that they weren't entitled to vote as their credentials hadn't yet come through from the union. Only the old guard could vote – the same members were re-elected, and Mrs Dibbs was re-elected for what was said to be her thirty-first year. The new stewards quickly grew frustrated with the Works Committee, and some wanted to drop out because they weren't getting anywhere. Rosemary was fed up with meetings that lasted after 4.15 and made her late for her 'part-time'.

The dispute lost us two weeks' wages, as well as reduced pay for the two weeks of go slow. It gained us 50p a week for two months. To our knowledge the 'anomalies' were never investigated. An attempt was made to remove the 50p when the two months were up. Eventually it was reinstated, and in the new self-financing productivity scheme an extra 10 points were added to the bonus scale so you could now earn a maximum bonus of £7 instead of £6. We felt let down by the other grades of workers who had been used against us through the productivity deal trick – they earned more than us in the first place, lost no money, and had benefited from our action.

At the end of November we threatened another go slow to try and secure the back-pay, but notices from management were distributed, informing us that this new scheme would 'give' each full-time worker £36 before Christmas, conditional on normal working. The same old tactic was being rolled out again, and, when its implications sunk in, there was a very stormy union meeting. All they were giving us was £12, the rest was the £3 a week productivity deal money added up for two months, and it was now conditional on 'good industrial relations' whereas it had originally been unconditional. We rejected the £12 on principle, and objected to the attempt to make us unpopular with the rest of the work force if we resumed the go slow. They wouldn't get the £3 at all if we did. At the same meeting, it emerged that the full-time IWTU official had been to management over our suspension money, and they had registered a 'failure to agree', which we interpreted as meaning that they had jointly decided to forget about it. This left us no room to manoeuvre – we just had to wait, as there wasn't any point in starting another go slow once the question of back-pay was in official hands. We felt we'd been tricked right along the line. The decisions were made behind closed doors, and we wondered if the whole thing had been planned in advance. The back-pay kept emotions high for months – much more than the original bonus claim.

Opposition to management remained entrenched. The women who had served on the pieceworkers' negotiating committee were horrified at the way the managers talked down to them and deliberately used long words. They were advised to stand up for themselves and 'just tell the men to speak plain English'. Some people were so demoralised by the outcome of the dispute that they thought it wasn't worth having started it. Others blamed the few who went back to work early, but most of the women were convinced that if we had stuck it out just a little bit longer we could have won.

The whole thing wasn't a complete failure. Our stewards were much better and eventually might have some say on the Works Committee. It gave us greater strength on the shopfloor to have more of them. People got to know each other better and we felt much closer to workers in other parts of the factory who had supported us. It marked a breakthrough in what the women dared do; they knew what tricks they'd have to look out for next time, and learnt how important it was for everyone to keep together. The knowledge that British Leyland had been affected made us aware of our strength, and we knew that a real stoppage would affect a large part of the motor industry all over the country. Next time, they would make sure everyone stuck it out together to the bitter end. Young women learnt how to speak at meetings and how to represent the others on their line, even though they were scared to take on the responsibility at first. After the initial demoralisation wore off, the dispute seemed to increase people's strength and self-confidence.

The pace of work was very hard between mid-November, when the dispute ended, and Christmas – presumably to make up for lost production. People got annoyed with each other over trivial matters, and we were generally depressed. I wouldn't let anyone put their jigs on 'my' flyover, and the others were just as irritable if someone disrupted the way they had arranged their bench. We broke down into ethnic groupings, the West Indian women blaming the Irish and the Irish blaming the Indians. Anna and Jill came and sat with me a lot. We were sick of hearing what the firm made out of us, and irritated with those women who had 'seen the light' after the event; it was too late, they were told, they should have stuck out for the £5 at the time, instead of harping on about it now. I felt demoralised as well, and for some days got really fed up when people came over to discuss 'what we should have done'.

The Works Committee trundled on. One day in January the boilers broke down and there was no heating. It was perishing cold in the shop, below the minimum temperature laid down by the Factory Act. Arthur Drury jollied us along saying that the harder we worked the warmer we'd get. We all put on our coats, and demanded that they mend the boilers. After a few hours, Mrs Dibbs took it up, but we were freezing by then. She negotiated a deal with management to give us an extra quarter-of-an-hour's break at lunchtime, and a 2p piece each to buy a hot drink. They said they'd get the heating on by the afternoon. Again this was all tricks: the canteen didn't open until 12 so there was no point in having an extra 15 minutes, and, as it was a Thursday and payday, they must have reckoned that if we stayed till lunchtime we'd stay all day because we wanted our money. As it was, the heating didn't come on at all that day, and the episode lost management and Mrs Dibbs another chunk of good will. We would have been within our legal rights to go home, but we didn't know that.

Chapter Nine
What to make of it?

Working in the factory dominated the rest of my life. I was so tired and had so little time that I needed the weekend to recuperate. I had little energy to go to meetings in the evening and was quickly irritated if they took more time than necessary or were conducted in an unbusinesslike way. There was no way I could keep up with my previous network of friends. Working permanently somewhere like UMEC would entail a complete change in my life-style – less free time, more regular domestic routine, and more centred on a smaller number of close friends.

In some ways I liked not having to decide what to do all the time, being able to forget about work in the evening, and watch television without feeling guilty. I felt much more rooted in social life – talking about the social contract with the women on the line seemed more meaningful than discussing it with radical intellectuals; current economic and political issues had a direct relevance to us. I became much more outgoing, and could chatter quite happily about this and that all day. I had to learn to express myself more concretely and to speak more quickly, for example when asked to explain where the extra came from when shares went up on the stock market from one day to the next. I learnt to translate tax forms into simple English and to write formal letters in a five-minute tea-break. It seemed as if I'd lived in slow motion until then. The work gave me an appreciation of the labour that goes into producing things; I looked at my iron, calculator and stereo in a new light, imagining how the pieces would have been put together by other low-paid women working on assembly lines.

In the months after the dispute I became more used to the work but gradually the repetition became harder to bear. At 8 in the morning the thought of checking another 500 UMOs that day left me reeling. All I could see when I looked up was a line of trays; in half an hour I'd have done all of them but the source was never ending. You never finished, and it was always the same. I had to invent more sums to make the time pass and try to daydream. I started eating sweets, again timed, every hour, then every half hour, just like Eileen and Josey, though normally I never touched them.

In the end I made a snap decision to leave and look for work in a similar factory but with better conditions – then I'd be able to think about that sort of job as a longer-term possibility. Rosemary said she'd follow me if I got a job at the higher-paid engineering factory on the Victoria Trading Estate. Leaving them all upset me. Arlene tried to persuade me to stay; I'd only find the same psychology amongst workers in other factories, she said, and if the pay was higher it must mean the work was harder. She wanted a photo of me. Alice heard from Arlene that I'd given in my notice – she was put out that I hadn't told her first. Every morning during my final week she counted the number of days 'to your freedom'. After I left I went back to visit several times, and I kept up with Rosemary and Doreen till they moved. I still go round to Anna and Frank's and come away with armfuls of vegetables and pots of jam. A year after leaving I bump into women from the sprocket shop or valve shop in the High Street. They remember me from the dispute and we stop for a chat. I often see Grace in Sainsbury's and Josey on the bus. Mrs Patel rushed across the road one Saturday to tell me she was emigrating to Canada.

When I left UMEC I couldn't have known quite how bad the employment situation had become. The personnel managers of most of the factories I had approached the previous summer sounded surprised that I was looking for factory work – because I was white and what they had to offer wasn't good enough for me in their eyes. This was after I'd scarcely opened my mouth, so I'm sure it had to do with race rather than class. The local labour market was clearly rigidly compartmentalised. Where conditions weren't too bad, the workers were white and labour turnover was low. Black and Asian women were concentrated in factories with lower pay and worse conditions and the labour turnover was consequently higher; the Asian women got the rock bottom of these jobs in the smallest factories and sweatshops. People seemed to apply only where they knew they were likely to get a job. The personnel manager of a large computer factory had said 'but you don't sound Asian' when I'd rung up about a job. When I said that I wasn't Asian he told me that there were only Indian women working in the factory 'and you wouldn't want to work with them, would you?'

It was quite different after nine months. I trudged round Victoria and the other trading estates for weeks and weeks but failed to get work. I tried everywhere. Every Tuesday I went to the sweet factory and to the American-owned food factory, but no jobs were going. The better-paid engineering factory only needed skilled workers and the personnel manager was very suspicious of me. Two trainee quality control jobs were advertised at a cosmetics factory, but when I asked about factory work, there was nothing doing – they suggested a clerical job. In recent years many of the factories on the Victoria Trading Estate had closed down completely, others had transferred production elsewhere and just retained warehouses or offices. I applied to two warehouses but was told they employed men only. I was offered only one job on the whole estate – at a factory manufacturing hi-fi equipment. This was one of the factories that appeared to have only black employees the previous summer. It was a quality control job, checking at the end of the line, for less money than I'd got at UMEC. You had to agree to body searches and they said the contract could be terminated at one hour's notice during the first month. I turned it down and tried further afield, but the only vacancies were much too far away.

Gradually I realised that I was more likely to be offered a job if I played up some of my qualifications, making it clear that I was white and had maths 'O' level. That got me the offer of the quality control jobs but I stood no chance at all of machine operating or assembly work because they could find heaps of women with much more experience than me.

I didn't want to work in a shop or office but applied out of desperation, only to find the same ethnic hierarchy. At the local Safeway in the High Street, the majority of assistants at that time were Asian women. The personnel manager told me about the hours, work and pay – you spent your day on the checkout till, he said, while shelf filling was done by other workers at night. I didn't have to fill in any forms. At Marks and Spencer on the other hand, I had to complete a long form, pass an arithmetic test and supply references. I was told that assistants were responsible for display and stocktaking on their counters as well as taking money. All the shop assistants I could see were white. Comparing the two shops, pay and conditions were better at Marks and Spencer, if you could stand the paternalism. The local Sainsbury's was in between: there were Irish, black and Asian women. You did shelf filling and labelling as well as sitting at the checkout, but the pay was only £39 for a 40-hour week – less than at UMEC.

Finally I tried London Transport, for bus conducting. As with Marks and Spencer, you had to fill in forms and go through several stages of interviews – they both took the pick of workers. In the 1950s and 1960s London Transport had relied heavily on immigrants and recruited directly in Barbados. But by 1978 there was nothing odd about ex-teachers applying for work on the buses. Most of the people queueing with me were white men, English and Irish. There were far fewer women, young or black people than I expected.

Altogether it seemed that when English women looked for work, they were not restricted to what local employers had to offer them – whether they were white women of any age or young women of Asian or Caribbean descent born or educated in Britain. Older women from the Indian sub-continent or the Caribbean, on the other hand, were restricted to a much narrower labour market, even if they had lived in West London for many years. The same applied to young women straight over from Ireland. Shop and office work in central London were by and large the preserve of English women, so long as they came up to the required standards of English or had clerical training. Oxford Circus is only half an hour from West London by underground, but local immigrant women looked for work within a very limited geographical area. They didn't extend their horizons beyond it – realistically – because they probably wouldn't have had much luck.

This situation helped to reinforce the rigid ethnic segregation and hierarchy which resulted in immigrant women being more confined than the others to local work, manual jobs and those with the lowest pay. White English women of all ages and young women of Irish descent appeared to get the best of the jobs for working-class women both locally and in central London. They were likely to get clerical work in offices and banks and better-paid shop work. Young women of Caribbean or Asian descent looked for the same sort of jobs as their white counterparts but with less success – no doubt informal racist employment policies discriminated against them. Certainly Arlene, Pearl and the other black women wouldn't allow their daughters to apply to UMEC. They were as qualified as any white girl.

After several months unemployment and much heart searching I returned – temporarily, I hoped – to teaching. Being out of work gave me the opportunity to reflect on the year as a whole and on some of the questions I had in mind before starting at UMEC. One of the things that had struck me most forcefully was how differently the younger women experienced life from middle-class girls of the same age. The job was a meal ticket – they didn't expect job satisfaction and couldn't consider it a career. They had to make the best of the little spare time they had, dressing up, going out drinking and dancing before they were tied down with a family and had to save. But marriage and children were also a way out of the factory. They had relatively little contact with the opposite sex, none at work, and they often went out with each other. There was no gap between the generations on the line – women of 50 talked to the 17-year-olds as equals. This made a change after teaching where one is acutely aware of age differences. Arlene and Josey for instance, had lots to discuss although Arlene's daughters were older than Josey.

There was no choice for the young girls but to make the best of it while they could. Once you'd left home you couldn't afford to live on the wages. None of them wanted to remain single and those who were had to supplement their wages by doing all the overtime they could or taking a part-time job as well. Life was equally hard for the mothers who worked: Sharon had to take and collect her small daughter from the child minder before and after work. Mrs Patel was up at 5 every day to do her housework, and Anna was not the only one who saw the two weeks' annual holiday as a chance to catch up with spring cleaning.

My understanding of the constraints on working-class women had been weak until I experienced them for myself and felt the same pressures towards conformity. It seemed only sensible to get married and benefit from the economies of scale of two wage packets. Given the wider job opportunities open to men and higher pay, swapping the role of husband and wife just wasn't on. The idea of the women going out to work and leaving the man at home to look after the children seemed mad to them – it would be economic suicide. Asking a husband to take an equal share of domestic responsibility would depend on being economically independent yourself or at least on a more equal footing money-wise; but this would be possible only if women's wages were higher, and more highly paid and skilled jobs were open to them.

The division between the sexes was well entrenched out-side work as well as inside, as is shown by the single-sex social life, closeness to other women, and views about what was fitting work or behaviour for men and women. Home and work were the two poles of their lives – linked by low pay. Together they formed a tight circle that would be hard to break. Doreen's reluctance to learn how to do traditionally 'male' jobs around the house seemed quite justified. She certainly wouldn't see any reason to change just because her views reflected her dependence on men. Pooling income with a man was the obvious way to live – you couldn't overcome married women's wages by ignoring them and choosing 'financial independence'. A home to relax in that you could call your own was about all you could hope for – it could almost make up for the work.

It was easy to understand why the women's lives and hopes revolved so completely round their home and family. Being low-skilled, low-paid workers outside the home, and shouldering the bulk of domestic responsibility within the family fitted together from both ends. Work, low pay, and home seemed more tightly linked for the women in the factory than for women in professional jobs. You could see how Doreen or Rosemary's outlook, aims in life, domestic arrangements and financial situation were all bound up with each other. A professional job with equal pay encourages you to expect some job satisfaction and to achieve something with your life. The shorter working week, higher pay and the fact of not being continually exhausted enable you to do more with your spare time, opening up the possibility of choosing how to conduct your life. But relationships at home and conditions at work were so bound together in a vicious circle for the women in the factory that, it seemed, to change anything at all in their lives you'd have to change everything.

Neither the women's movement nor any other political grouping is in a position to even attempt to affect all the different spheres of life at present. But if we are not just to give up at the size of the task, what can we aim for in the meantime? The most obvious immediate priorities for working-class women would seem to be the shortening of the working week, better nursery provision, shops staying open later, fighting equal pay cases, demanding equal job opportunities for girls, and a whole host of other practical changes.

The basic demands of the Women's Liberation Movement for equal pay and opportunities, day-care for children and provision of free contraception and abortion would benefit all women. But our discussions about 'alternatives to the family' and 'changing relationships' reflected the outlook of a specific group of women – mostly young, white, single, childless and professional, women in a position to try and take control of our own lives, and to decide how we wanted to live. We might not have been able to put our wishes into practice, but at least we could think about it. It seemed more feasible to attack the issues separately with the possibility of making some progress.

Campaigns about 'determining our own sexuality', important though they are, would have no immediate relevance to the women I worked with. The future was already mapped out for Jill, Josey and Rosemary. In a few years they would marry and have children. Freely available contraception and abortion would help them control when to get pregnant and how often, but childcare provision would probably be even more important. Women's movement discussions about living independently of men or choosing not to have children wouldn't make much sense. If a 19 year old like Maureen has a baby it's not because she disapproves of abortion or can't plan ahead. She just has a completely different outlook on what her life is about and what she can hope to achieve from it than most active feminists. She's not going to achieve any-thing in her work, and she's going to have children at some stage, so why not now?

Rosemary, Arlene and the others were familiar with every-thing I came out with from the women's movement. They knew why men were more highly trained and had more power than them, and why we were paid married women's wages. Many told stories of women going mad, and treatment at the hands of doctors and mental hospitals that tried to keep them quiet with tranquillisers – accounts you could have expected in a women's movement consciousness-raising group. Their whole experience of life had been more affected by the division between the sexes than mine. This had made them conscious of themselves as women and dependent on other women for company and support. As teenagers Josey and Maureen were already pretty jaded about men, and had few illusions about the possible relationship between the sexes. They wouldn't have used the word 'sexism', but they knew exactly what it meant.

The reason we haven't attracted working-class women to the women's movement is not that they aren't feminist or are unaware. Our discussions are too up in the air for them and reflect a very different way of life. When you do hard physical work for 8 hours and housework on top, you aren't inclined to go to meetings in the evening – especially with people you don't know and about campaigns that may not come to fruition for years. Grace and several of the others were in tenants' organisations, but they'd be unlikely to get involved in other campaigns unless the meetings addressed their needs directly and discussed the problems on their terms. Unless it changes drastically, the women's movement may remain primarily a movement of middle-class women and a servicing organisation for working-class women, agitating for facilities that will benefit them, but without their active participation. This is not to put it down – we were probably naïve in expecting working-class women to become involved.

The pressures to 'make do' at home and at work were very, very strong. Alice knew that you could make the work harder by making a fuss, and so unpacked her transistors during the tea-break. It was difficult to do only the number of trays necessary to reach our basic wage, even when we knew how the bonus system was organised. It took great effort and courage, as well as financial hardship, to challenge work conditions. Everyone understood the situation and what was called for – no one accepted it passively. The odds were so stacked against us that in some ways the dispute was doomed from the start. Yet, most of the women saw it through and were prepared to speak out and let management know what they thought of them despite the possible consequences. The militancy and solidarity lasted throughout the dispute and showed what they could do if they stuck it out together. Afterwards they were less prepared to make do, although it would take many disputes to change things in the factory.

Involvement in the dispute showed that the women were more likely to take action on their own behalf at work than outside. Here they were brought together daily under the same conditions, and had a collective awareness of being exploited. The first step in organising was to call a meeting at the back of the line – it's much harder to know where to begin organising outside of work where women are more isolated from one another. The solidarity that grew out of the shared experience is what gave the women strength and self-confidence.

I've stressed how sexual division affects all areas of life for the women who worked on the line, making their experience quite different from men's. How does this relate to divisions in the work force at UMEC? Is the sexual division a class division as well?

There was no common experience of working on the shop floor. Workers in different grades were separated by their specialisms, place in the hierarchy, and particular pay and conditions. Operators did only manual work tied to the line, while the chargehands' and supervisors' administrative responsibilities involved walking around to oversee the work. The engineers' tasks were technical, and more high-powered. Looking at the hierarchy from the position of a woman operator, there was a very basic divide between those who ran the line and those who were run by it – the engineers and supervisors firmly on one side, and us on the other. We did the hardest work and got the worst deal.

The supervisors' perks were at our expense, and you could never imagine them taking our side against the firm. We felt loyal only to our own grade, and no doubt they did too. Arthur Drury's authority over us, and our two-sided relationship with Reg weren't just personal. They arose from the division of labour and the organisation of the work. Resisting their power over the clock was important – otherwise they could gradually impose worse conditions. In the long run, though, it was the relations of production underlying their authority that would have to be challenged.

The division of labour was reinforced by divisions of sex and race. The separation of women's work from men's work was the most obvious, but amongst the men, white English men were concentrated at the top, black and Asian men at the bottom, and Irish men somewhere in between.

I still feel a long way from being able to combine a theoretical understanding of class with a proper concrete analysis. Even my understanding of the different groupings amongst the workers was that of an outsider. It would have taken years of working at UMEC to be able to read the signs correctly and know which groups would ally with each other and under what circumstances. While I was there, the issues that arose were specific to one group of workers only, pieceworkers or supervisors, and there was little support from the others. Maybe there are issues that would unite them all, but intuitively I thought it would have to be something major, like a threat of redundancy, affecting all grades of workers. As it was, the other manual workers might line up with the women but the chargehands and quality controllers wavered between supporting us and the supervisors.

Thinking about class categories from outside the factory, one might be tempted to lump all the types and grades of production workers together in one homogeneous group of wage labourers. But working inside the factory I had to face the fact that the differences seemed almost to override the similarities, and a theory of class could not ignore that. Of course, everyone was part of the working class in the sense of selling their labour power in return for a wage, but the groups were in a specific relation to production according to their place in the division of labour. By division of labour I mean the broad groups of workers with varying types and levels of skill, technical expertise and work conditions, to be found at the different rungs in the hierarchy. I'm not talking here about the detailed technical division of labour which operated even on the line where the women carried out only their own specialised task.

One effect of the rigid division of labour was to place each group in a specific relation to the process of production, with implications, for example, on the way surplus value was extracted from them. For the women on the line the firm's productivity and profits depended directly on line speed, how frequently the light flashed and how many trays of UMOs we assembled each day. One could say that the rate of extraction of surplus value from us was directly proportional to the physical and mental intensity of our pace of work. This was not so for the chargehands and even less for the supervisors, none of whom were tied to the line. As direct producers, the women on the line and the machine shop workers received a piecework wage, its size varying with how much was produced. Supervisors were not direct producers and had no piecework element in their wage. Surplus value extracted from their labour could not depend on their output, nor on the actual intensity of their work. They were paid a set rate for the job; the chargehands, however, did receive a bonus element dependent on the performance achieved by the women on their line.

Our demands over the bonus were specific to pieceworkers. None of the other groups was subject to such a bonus system, so the issue didn't draw them in. Indeed, the less fuss we made, the easier life was for the supervisors. That is why it is difficult to imagine issues that would unite all of the workers on the shopfloor.

Changes in the organisation of production showed how management was constantly looking for ways to boost pro- duction at no extra cost. The introduction of materials feeders and the regrading of chargehands was an example of tampering with the management structure to find the most economical and efficient method of shopfloor supervision.

The connection between work intensity and extraction of surplus value is one example of the different relation to production of the different grades. The division of labour lies at the root of this – it doesn't create different classes but it does influence the position of the different groups within the working class, and plays an important part in class strucuturing. It doesn't override the basic distinction between the labour and capital, but it means that labour can't be viewed simply as one large homogeneous group.

Turning from the division of labour within the production process, to the conditions under which people sell their labour in the first place, it would again be wrong to lump everyone together just because they sell their labour power in return for a wage. Both top managers and labourers for example had to sell their labour in order to live. But they sold it on the labour market under very different conditions.

When people look for work they already have a particular type of labour power to sell, more or less skilled and more or less valuable. In general, women and immigrants sell their labour under much less favourable conditions than skilled white men. In any case the division of labour presupposes the existence of various types of labour power with differing degrees of skill and training; the work process is based on them and reinforces them.

Historically, women's responsibility for childrearing and domestic labour have resulted in very limited access to skills and training for paid employment outside the home. In the past, women were assumed to be economically dependent on their husbands and employed only temporarily – before or after having children. Little investment has been made in equipping them with the formal training required at higher levels of the division of labour; they would provide a poor return in comparison with the continuous working life of a man. So women have fewer formal skills to offer employers, and a less valuable sort of labour power to sell. Hence, the concentration of married women in routine and semi-skilled work, and their low wages.

For people who come to England from overseas*, the causes are different but the effect is similar. British imperialism has left massive unemployment in most of its ex-colonies. The West Indies, India and Ireland are much less industrialised than Britain, and there is not the same sort of education system creating all the different layers and levels of labour with their various skills. Whenever there's been full employment here, making British workers more costly, employers have made use of the large pool of cheaper unskilled workers abroad. Unemployment at home and the prospect of work over here have in turn encouraged West Indians, Asians, and Irish people to emigrate to Britain.

Women and immigrants both represent cheap labour used in the least skilled jobs, so reserving the higher reaches of skill and pay for white English men. So differential access to education is fundamental in forming the different types of labour power. But all workers are not equal on the labour market for a second important reason: their availability and mobility. For example, whatever level of skill a woman has, she may not be continuously available for employment in the same way as a man, which puts her at a disadvantage. Likewise, newly arrived immigrants often rely on friends and relatives to help fix them up with a job if they haven't been recruited raw at home by the company, and this dependence restricts their mobility.

UMEC had a definite recruitment policy – at one time it

* When I refer to immigrant labour in the next few pages, I am talking about people who themselves emigrated to Britain, from Ireland or any other part of the world. Most black and Asian people in Britain today are not immigrants – they were born here, and these comments aren't intended to be about black and Asian people in general. I didn't meet any young black or Asian women at UMEC and would guess that racism in the labour market affected them differently – but not necessarily any less – than their parents as I explained when discussing the local and wider employment structure.

recruited directly in Ireland, presumably because cheap labour was scarce here and plentiful there. Now there is no need for that with cheap female immigrant labour available locally, and increasing youth unemployment. Employing immediate school leavers would have certain advantages from the firm's point of view: the youth rate made under-eighteens 'economical' and they would already be accustomed to an 8-hour day and work discipline from school. They would probably pick up the jobs quicker than older Asian or West Indian women especially those who hadn't worked outside the home before. It seemed 'rational' for the firm to take on Jill, or Josey and her friends in preference to Mrs Patel who hadn't worked in England before and whose lack of English made her slow at following instructions. Even if Josey and her mates were loud, unruly and had little respect for the line, they could work quickly when they got down to it. The sort of women UMEC looked for changed over time with the changing labour supply but their aim must always have been to employ the most reliable unskilled labour willing to work for the price.

From what I hear, the English school leavers didn't last long and UMEC turned to young girls of Asian origin instead. White English girls probably had a better chance of office work. Josey would warn her friends against applying to UMEC. They'd get office work if they waited long enough. But Rosemary's first reaction when Geraldine arrived without any money was to fix her up with a job on the line. Many of the Irish girls had heard of UMEC from friends who'd worked there, and came over knowing jobs would be available. Mrs Patel knew most of the other Indian women before she started. UMEC relied on this local network of immigrant women who were familiar with the job structure and knew where they were most likely to get work. It was a constant source of labour for the factory, and self-replenishing, because the women told friends and relatives here and at home that UMEC was looking for women.

Class is a relation, in this case a relation between wage labour and capital. Consequently, differences in the relation between wage labour and capital are of a class nature. But at the same time there are definite divisions within the working class as a whole; workers cannot all be placed in an equal and identical relation of wage labour to capital. White, male engineers are certainly not a separate class, exploiting women or immigrants. They share a common subordination to capital, and their labour is exploited. But their relation to capital, both in the conditions of sale of their labour power and in the labour process, is very different from that of unskilled women just over from Ireland.

I don't want to suggest that UMEC was a microcosm of British industry; its work force and work process were not typical, but the result of local historical factors. Certainly the concentration of women workers in semi-skilled manual and lower clerical grades is characteristic of British industry as a whole, but the rigid ethnic subdivisions of UMEC's occupational hierarchy are linked with the specific conditions of the West London factory. Cheap labour has permitted UMEC to continue operating with old-fashioned labour-intensive methods of production. If labour had been scarce, they would have had more incentive to modernise. However, installing new machinery would have been expensive and made the production process more capital intensive. More advanced technology would also have required a different sort of labour force, more highly skilled and hence more expensive.

I doubt that you would find exactly the same ethnic divisions between women workers in other parts of the country. Shop and office work in Central London, and the large immigrant population in West London must have skewed the local labour market. The small number of skilled manual workers – men – was another particular feature of UMEC's work force, though this could also be characteristic of semi-skilled assembly industries. There would have been more jobs for skilled workers only if production methods had been more advanced, which would have meant fewer jobs for unskilled women. As it happens skilled engineering workers are in short supply locally, and adverts in the papers offer them the 'best' conditions and 'most competitive' rates of pay, almost double ours.

All in all, the production process at UMEC and the type of labour it required depended on each other and determined each other. There is no essential need for assembly work to be so labour intensive. In America industrial robots have been developed to assemble UMOs and already 'work' alongside women on the line at General Motors. According to their manufacturers, they can perform certain repetitive operations with greater precision than humans. Other companies in the UMEC group are famous for developing and using the latest advances in technology. So the policy of using cheap labour and low technology must be more profitable than modernising, despite high labour turnover and high absenteeism.

I wouldn't want to make too much of these comments: they're not intended as a general conclusion but rather to show how I came to look at these questions while working in the factory. The experience changed me and my political outlook, challenging my understanding of the relation between race, sex and class and of the different groups within wage labour. It also showed me that we would need to build a new relation between intellectuals and the working class in order to deepen this understanding.

D